SIMPLE
FOOD
4 YOU

SIMPLE FOOD 4 YOU

Life-Saving 30-Minute Recipes
for Happier Weeknight Meals

ALEXANDRA JOHNSSON

Creator of Simple Food 4 You

PAGE STREET
PUBLISHING CO.

First published in 2023 by
Page Street Publishing Co.
27 Congress Street, Suite 1511
Salem, MA 01970

www.pagestreetpublishing.com

Distributed by Macmillan, sales in Canada by The Canadian Manda Group.

27   26   25   24   23   1   2   3   4   5

ISBN-13: 978-1-64567-716-1
ISBN-10: 1-64567-716-8

Library of Congress Control Number: 2022941256

Cover and book design by Kylie Alexander for Page Street Publishing Co.
Photography by Toni Zernik

Printed and bound in China

TO MY FAMILY,
WHO IS ALWAYS THERE FOR ME.
THANK YOU FOR YOUR CONSTANT LOVE
AND SUPPORT, AND FOR PUTTING UP WITH
MY HANGRY TEMPER WHEN I HAVEN'T EATEN.
I LOVE YOU.

TABLE OF CONTENTS

INTRODUCTION

Late in 2020, my cooking journey, which until then had just been taking place in my kitchen in a small Swedish town, started for real. I began sharing my cooking on my TikTok, @simplefood4you, and I would have never thought the response would be as great as it was. It was overwhelming! Ever since then, I've continued creating cooking content and sharing new recipes, and today I have more than 2 million followers from all over the world re-creating my recipes and sharing my videos.

But who am I? I'm a 30-year-old self-taught chef who's always been passionate about cooking and trying new flavors. Ever since I was a little kid, I've been traveling around the world with my family, and that has allowed me to try a lot of different kinds of food. You'll recognize this in my recipes, as they contain flavors from many different countries.

This book contains 60 simple recipes that you can put together in 30 minutes or less. The main thing that I want to communicate with my cooking is that making great food doesn't have to be hard. This book is all about maximum flavor and minimum effort. I've always said that cooking should be simple and fun, and I believe that everyone can cook when given the right conditions. My goal is to inspire people to get into cooking, love the process as much as the result and feel confident trying new things.

These recipes are as great for a stressful weeknight as they are for the weekend when inviting friends and family over. Why not turn cooking into a fun activity and spend time with your loved ones in the kitchen? I hope this book will be useful and that you love these recipes as much as I do.

I'd love to see you make my recipes! Don't forget to tag @simplefood4you on TikTok and Instagram when cooking.

BEST OF TORTILLAS

Tortillas have become my signature ingredient when cooking on TikTok and Instagram. The Chicken Fold Wrap (page 12) even started a tortilla trend all over social media. And I get why everyone is crazy about these tortilla dishes. They're simple, fun and delicious. I love the idea of using tortillas in my cooking because you can make so many different things with them, and the options of ingredients to add are endless.

CHICKEN FOLD WRAP

Prep: 10 min
Cook: 15 to 20 min
Total: 25 to 30 min
Servings: 2

Ingredients
8 ounces (226 g) store-bought frozen chicken fingers or chicken nuggets

4 slices bacon

2 large flour tortillas

1 avocado, sliced

4 thin slices tomato

1/8 red onion, thinly sliced

4 tablespoons (60 ml) Jalapeño Spread (page 75)

2/3 cup (74 g) shredded mozzarella cheese

When I first made this wrap, it quickly became my most viewed TikTok video. Today it still is, with more than 80 million views. TikTok even announced that this was the most viewed video in Sweden in 2021. Without knowing it, I started a "tortilla trend" and saw people all over the world re-create this wrap. I still make this all the time, and you'll never get tired of it because you can substitute ingredients and make this wrap in so many different ways. I've turned it into a taco wrap, a burger wrap and also a pizza wrap.

Instructions
Heat the chicken fingers according to package instructions.

Meanwhile, place the bacon in a large pan and cook it over high heat. When the bacon starts to sizzle, reduce the heat to medium-high, and continue cooking until the bacon is crispy, 3 to 4 minutes. Remove the bacon from the pan, and place it on a paper towel or a rack to drain.

Place 1 tortilla on a clean, flat surface, and use a knife or scissors to make a cut from the bottom of the tortilla straight up to the center of the tortilla. In the bottom-left corner of the tortilla (to the left of the cut), place half of the avocado and 2 slices of bacon. In the top-left corner, add half of the tomato and half of the red onion. In the top-right corner, place 2 tablespoons (30 ml) of Jalapeño Spread, and place half of the chicken on top (you might have to cut and shape the chicken a little to fit it in the corner). In the bottom-right corner (to the right of the cut), add half of the mozzarella cheese.

Starting on the corner with the avocado and bacon, place your thumbs underneath the tortilla and lift it toward the upper-left corner. Use your other fingers to hold the avocado and bacon in place while folding them over the tomato and red onion. Now, holding this together, fold the top-left corner (which is now folded once already) over the chicken (top-right corner). Hold the whole thing together while folding it down one more time over the mozzarella cheese. The whole tortilla should now be folded into one triangle-shaped wrap. Repeat with the second tortilla.

Carefully place the wraps into a panini maker, and cook until golden brown, about 5 minutes.

Note: If you don't have a panini maker, you can use a frying pan. Cook the wraps for about 4 minutes on each side over medium-low heat.

SALMON WRAP WITH AVOCADO AND EGG SALAD

Prep: 15 min
Cook: 15 min
Total: 30 min
Servings: 2

Egg Salad

2 hard-boiled eggs, mashed

2 tablespoons (20 g) finely chopped red onion (about ¼ red onion)

½ cup (120 ml) mayonnaise

⅛ teaspoon salt

⅛ teaspoon garlic powder

¼ teaspoon lemon pepper (see Note)

Wrap

7 ounces (200 g) fully cooked smoke-roasted salmon (see Note)

2 large flour tortillas

2 cups (94 g) shredded lettuce

1 avocado, thinly sliced

This salmon wrap makes a simple, light lunch that's perfect on the go. I'm always looking for new lunch recipes that are easy to take to work and, with this one, you don't even have to spend time in line for the microwave. Even though I love fish, I always end up making wraps with chicken but, after creating this recipe, it is definitely a go-to for me. Salmon, egg and avocado are the perfect combination!

Instructions

In a medium-sized bowl, combine the mashed hard-boiled eggs, red onion, mayonnaise, salt, garlic powder and lemon pepper, and set aside. On a separate plate, use a fork to mash up the salmon.

Heat the tortillas in the microwave for 10 to 15 seconds until soft, and place them on a clean, flat surface.

In a line down the center of each tortilla, add half of the lettuce. Divide the salmon and egg salad into two equal parts. Place one part salmon and one part egg salad on top of the lettuce, followed by half of the avocado slices.

Fold the sides over the filling, like you are wrapping a burrito. Roll the tortilla over the filling, and tuck it in as you roll. Continue rolling until it's all wrapped up.

Notes: If you don't have lemon pepper, you can substitute with ¼ teaspoon of black pepper and ¼ teaspoon of lemon juice.

You can substitute the smoke-roasted salmon for fried salmon or drained canned tuna.

CHEESY DOUBLE-CRUNCH TACOS WITH HOMEMADE PICO DE GALLO

Prep: 15 min
Cook: 15 min
Total: 30 min
Servings: 4 (8 small tacos)

Pico de Gallo (makes 1¼ cup)
1 cup (149 g) finely chopped tomato

2 tablespoons (20 g) finely chopped yellow onion

2 tablespoons (20 g) finely chopped pickled jalapeños

1 tablespoon (1 g) finely chopped fresh cilantro leaves

1 tablespoon (15 ml) lime juice (about ½ lime)

⅛ teaspoon salt

Tacos
9 ounces (255 g) ground beef

2 tablespoons (28 g) taco seasoning

8 hard taco shells

1 cup (47 g) finely shredded lettuce

½ cup (120 ml) Taco Sauce (page 23)

8 small flour tortillas

4 cups (452 g) shredded Cheddar cheese

Almost everything tastes better with more cheese. Add a soft tortilla and some Cheddar cheese, and it'll take your ordinary taco to a whole new level, without needing a lot of extra effort from you. And this homemade pico de gallo is the key to boosting the flavor of this recipe.

Instructions

In a medium-sized bowl, combine the tomato, onion, pickled jalapeños, cilantro, lime juice and salt. Refrigerate the pico de gallo while you prepare the rest of the ingredients for the tacos.

Heat a large pan over medium-high heat. Add the ground beef and cook, breaking up the meat, until brown, about 6 minutes. Mix in the taco seasoning.

Fill each taco shell with 3 tablespoons (42 g) of ground beef, 2 tablespoons (8 g) of shredded lettuce, 1 tablespoon (15 ml) of Taco Sauce and 2 tablespoons (32 g) of pico de gallo.

Place the tortillas on a clean, flat surface, and spread ½ cup (57 g) of the Cheddar over each tortilla. Heat the tortillas in the microwave for about 30 seconds or until the cheese is melted. If preferred, you can place the tortillas on a baking sheet and heat them in the oven (400°F [200°C]) for 5 minutes or until the cheese is melted.

Place a hard taco standing up in the center of each tortilla, and fold the sides of the tortilla up over the outside of the hard shell.

16   Simple Food 4 You

EVERYDAY CHICKEN WRAP WITH HOME-MADE AVOCADO-RANCH DRESSING

Prep: 10 min
Cook: 20 min
Total: 30 min
Servings: 4

Ingredients
1 teaspoon paprika

1 teaspoon garlic powder

½ teaspoon salt

½ teaspoon ground black pepper

13 ounces (364 g) boneless, skinless chicken breast, thinly sliced

8 slices bacon

4 large flour tortillas

2 cups (94 g) finely shredded lettuce

12 thin slices tomato

½ red onion, thinly sliced

4 tablespoons (38 g) feta cheese crumbles

1 cup (240 ml) Avocado–Ranch Dressing (page 85)

Wraps are so simple to make and a perfect lunch on the go. This is a wrap that I can eat every single day and never get tired of. The soft flour tortilla is packed with juicy chicken, fresh crispy vegetables and a creamy avocado–ranch dressing.

Instructions

In a small bowl, mix the paprika, garlic powder, salt and pepper together.

In a large bowl, add the sliced chicken. Sprinkle the seasoning over the chicken, and use your hands to combine until the chicken is covered with the spices.

Place the bacon in a large pan and heat over high heat. When the bacon starts to sizzle, reduce the heat to medium-high, and continue cooking until the bacon is crispy, 3 to 4 minutes, stirring frequently. Remove the bacon from the pan, and place it on a paper towel to drain. Once cool, chop the bacon and set aside.

In the same pan over medium-high heat, cook the chicken in the bacon fat for 3 to 4 minutes until the chicken is cooked through, then remove the pan from the heat.

Place the tortillas on a clean, flat surface. In a line down the center of each tortilla, add a quarter of the lettuce, tomato, red onion, chicken, bacon, feta cheese crumbles and dressing. Wrap the tortillas up by folding the bottom over the ingredients, followed by the two sides, leaving the top part open.

Note: The avocado–ranch dressing is also great for any type of salad.

TACO LASAGNA

Prep: 5 min
Cook: 30 min
Total: 35 min
Servings: 4 to 6

Ingredients

14 ounces (392 g) ground beef

4 tablespoons (56 g) taco seasoning

5¼ ounces (152 g) cream cheese

5 tablespoons (75 ml) salsa

1 cup (149 g) finely chopped tomato

⅔ cup (70 g) finely chopped yellow onion

4½ ounces (127 g) canned corn, drained

3 medium-sized flour tortillas

12 nacho chips

6 tablespoons (57 g) feta cheese crumbles

1½ cups (169 g) shredded mozzarella or Cheddar cheese, plus more for garnish

Note: I like to serve my lasagna with a side of chopped lettuce and my homemade guacamole (page 130).

This is the first recipe I ever posted on my TikTok and the dish that got this whole journey started for me. The response made me continue cooking for you and growing as a content creator. As the title suggests, this is kind of like a lasagna with its different layers, but with taco ingredients in between tortillas. I use taco leftovers for this recipe, which makes it so easy. The recipe calls for ingredients I like in my taco, but the varieties of what you can use are endless.

Instructions

Preheat the oven to 430°F (220°C).

Heat a large pan over medium-high heat. Add the ground beef and cook, breaking up the meat, until brown, about 6 minutes. Mix in the taco seasoning. If you have leftover taco meat, you can skip this step and heat that up.

Add the cream cheese and salsa, and cook, stirring to combine, 1 to 2 minutes. Remove from the heat.

In a medium-sized bowl, combine the tomato, onion and corn.

Spray the bottom of a 9-inch (23-cm) springform pan with removable sides with cooking spray. Place 1 tortilla in the bottom of the pan, and spread a third of the ground beef mixture all over the tortilla, followed by a third of the tomato mixture.

Using your hands, crumble 4 nacho chips, and spread them out on top of the vegetables, then add 2 tablespoons (19 g) of the feta cheese crumbles on top.

Spread out ½ cup (56 g) of the mozzarella cheese over the feta, followed by a second tortilla. Repeat with the remaining ingredients for two more layers. Finish the last layer with shredded cheese.

Bake for 15 minutes. Once the lasagna is done, remove the sides of the springform pan, and use a sharp knife to cut into wedges.

TACO CRUNCH WRAP

Prep: 5 to 10 min
Cook: 20 min
Total: 25 to 30 min
Servings: 4

Taco Sauce
½ cup (120 ml) sour cream

4 teaspoons (18 g) taco seasoning

Wrap
14 ounces (392 g) ground beef

3 tablespoons (42 g) taco seasoning

4 large flour tortillas

24–32 triangle nacho chips (or 4 crispy tostada shells), divided

¾ cup (150 g) Addictive Guacamole (page 130), divided

4 tablespoons (40 g) chopped pickled jalapeños, divided

3 cups (336 g) shredded Cheddar cheese, divided

4 small flour tortillas

I've seen a lot of people post on social media about Taco Bell's Crunchwrap®, and let me say, it looks delicious! Since we don't have Taco Bell in Sweden, I decided to make my own version of it at home. The creaminess from my special sauce together with the guacamole, the crunch from nacho chips and the heat from the jalapeños make the perfect combination.

Instructions

In a medium-sized bowl, combine the sour cream and taco seasoning and set aside.

In a large pan over medium-high heat, cook the ground beef, breaking up the meat, until brown, about 6 minutes. Add the taco seasoning and mix.

Place 1 large tortilla on a clean, flat surface, and spread 2 tablespoons (30 ml) of the taco sauce in the center of the tortilla, making a circle the size of a small tortilla. Add a quarter of the ground beef on top of the taco sauce. Repeat with the remaining tortillas, sauce and beef.

Place 6 to 8 of the nacho chips on top of the ground beef with the tip of the triangles facing the middle point, until they've made a circle, or add a tostada shell. Add 3 tablespoons (38 g) of guacamole, 1 tablespoon (10 g) of chopped jalapeños and ¾ cup (84 g) of shredded cheese on top of the nacho chips.

Put 1 small tortilla on top of the cheese to create a lid, and fold part of the edge of the large tortilla toward the top and center of the small tortilla. Use your other hand to hold the small tortilla in place, and keep working your way around until the large tortilla is closed around the small one. Carefully flip the tortilla (while holding it together) so that the folded part is facing down, which will keep it from opening back up. Repeat with all the wraps.

Heat two large frying pans over medium-low heat, and place two wraps in each pan, folded sides facing down. Cook until golden brown, about 4 minutes on each side. Remove, cut in half and serve.

CRISPY TORTILLA WRAPS WITH CHICKEN FILLING

Prep: 10 min
Cook: 15 min
Total: 25 min
Servings: 4

Ingredients

1 cup (240 ml) plain whole-milk full-fat Greek yogurt

6 tablespoons (90 ml) Thai sweet chili sauce

½ teaspoon garlic powder

3 tablespoons (9 g) chopped green onion

3 ounces (84 g) canned corn, drained

2 cups (224 g) shredded mozzarella and Cheddar cheese mix

¼ teaspoon salt

¾ teaspoon ground black pepper

16 ounces (448 g) rotisserie chicken, skin and bones removed

4 large flour tortillas

This chicken wrap is so easy to make for lunch or dinner during the week. Its hot and sweet flavors from the sweet chili sauce together with the melted cheese and crispy tortilla make it delicious! This is a favorite among both kids and grown-ups in my family, and I'm sure it'll be a new favorite of yours as well.

Instructions

In a large bowl, combine the yogurt, chili sauce, garlic powder, green onion, corn, cheese mix, salt, pepper and chicken.

Heat a tortilla in the microwave for 10 to 15 seconds to soften.

Place the tortilla on a clean, flat surface, and spread a quarter of the chicken mixture in the center of the tortilla, making a square (about 4 inches [10 cm] across). Fold the left and right sides of the tortilla over the filling toward the center so the sides overlap. Repeat with the bottom and top sides while holding the already-folded sides in place with the other hand. The tortilla should now cover all the filling.

Carefully flip the tortilla (while holding it together) so that the folded part is facing down, which will keep it from opening back up. Repeat with the rest of the tortillas and remaining ingredients.

Heat two large frying pans over medium-low heat. Place two wraps in each pan, folded sides down. Cook until they're golden brown, about 4 minutes. Then carefully flip and cook on the other side for 4 minutes more. Serve sliced diagonally.

SIMPLE FAJITA QUESADILLAS

Prep: 10 min
Cook: 20 min
Total: 30 min
Servings: 2

Fajita Spice Mix
1 teaspoon paprika
1 teaspoon ground cumin
½ teaspoon chili powder
½ teaspoon onion powder
¼ teaspoon ground black pepper
¼ teaspoon dried oregano
½ teaspoon salt
¼ teaspoon light brown sugar

Quesadilla
8 ounces (226 g) chicken breasts, thinly sliced
1 tablespoon (15 ml) extra virgin olive oil, divided
½ small yellow onion, thinly sliced
½ small red bell pepper, thinly sliced
2 large flour tortillas
1 cup (112 g) grated mozzarella or Cheddar cheese

Here we have the Mexican classics: fajita and quesadilla all in one. Soft tortillas filled with flavorful chicken, vegetables and melted cheese, and fried crispy. Cooking definitely doesn't have to be hard, and these are so easy to put together. I recommend serving them with a side of my homemade guacamole (page 130).

Instructions

In a small bowl, combine the paprika, cumin, chili powder, onion powder, pepper, oregano, salt and brown sugar.

In a large bowl, combine the chicken and spice mixture, using your hands to rub the spices into the chicken until it is well covered.

Add half of the olive oil in a large pan, and heat over medium heat. Add the onion and pepper, and cook, stirring occasionally, until they start to soften, about 4 minutes. Remove from the heat, and transfer the onion mixture to a bowl.

In the same pan over medium-high heat, add the remaining olive oil and the chicken. Cook until the chicken is cooked all the way through, 3 to 4 minutes. Add the cooked vegetables into the pan with the chicken, toss and turn off the heat.

Place 1 tortilla in another large pan, and turn the heat on medium-low. While the pan is heating, sprinkle half of the cheese over the tortilla. Add all the chicken and vegetables on top and spread them out evenly. Add the rest of the cheese on top.

Place the second tortilla on top, and use either your hand or a spatula to press it down a little. When the bottom tortilla is golden brown, after 5 to 6 minutes, carefully flip the whole thing so that the tortilla that was on top is facing the pan. Keep pressing down on the top of the tortilla every now and then. Cook until the tortilla facing the pan is golden brown, about 3 minutes more, then remove and place it on a cutting board. Cut the tortilla in half (one half per person), and then cut each half into two to four slices.

MY FAVORITE PASTAS

What's better than a meal that's simple to make, packed with flavors and good for your wallet? These pasta dishes are great for a weeknight dinner but are also elegant enough to serve at any occasion. A creamy pasta is always a safe choice, and these recipes will impress all your friends and family.

SIMPLE PESTO PASTA

Prep: 5 min
Cook: 10 to 15 min
Total: 10 to 20 min
Servings: 2

Pasta
6 ounces (170 g) uncooked penne

Pesto (makes ½ cup [120 ml])
5 tablespoons [40 g] pine nuts or chopped walnuts, divided

1 cup (24 g) fresh basil leaves

½ cup (33 g) freshly grated Parmesan cheese, plus more for garnish

1 clove garlic, peeled

⅛ teaspoon salt

½ teaspoon ground black pepper

½ tablespoon (8 ml) lemon juice

¼ cup (60 ml) extra virgin olive oil

Did you know that before 2020 I had never tried pesto? I quickly realized that I had been missing out. And even though the store-bought pesto I've tried is great, nothing beats this homemade one. Making pesto is really simple. This recipe will save you on any stressful day, and let it serve as a reminder that impressive recipes don't have to take hours to make.

Instructions
Bring a pot of salted water to boil, and cook the penne according to box instructions. Before draining, reserve 2 tablespoons (30 ml) of the pasta water.

Heat a small pan over low heat, and add the pine nuts. Toast the pine nuts until light brown, about 5 minutes, stirring often, and set aside.

While the penne is cooking, make the pesto. In a blender or food processor, combine the basil, pine nuts (reserving 2½ tablespoons [20 g] for garnish), Parmesan, garlic, salt, pepper and lemon juice, and blend on high speed until combined, about 15 seconds.

Reduce the speed to very low, and slowly add the olive oil. Turn the blender off as soon as you've added all the olive oil (blending the olive oil too fast or for too long will make the pesto taste bitter). If you don't have a blender or a food processor, you can blend the pesto by hand using a mortar and pestle.

In a large bowl, add the pesto and pasta water, and mix. Add the drained pasta and toss.

Plate the pesto pasta on two plates and top it off with more Parmesan and the rest of the toasted pine nuts.

Notes: This pesto recipe is great for my Grilled Pesto and Mozzarella Sandwich (page 68).

I use a bowl to toss the pasta with the pesto because if you add the pesto to the pasta pot, the residual heat will cause the basil to darken and the flavor to be bitter.

CREAMY MUSHROOM PASTA

Prep: 5 min
Cook: 15 min
Total: 20 min
Servings: 2

Ingredients

6 ounces (170 g) penne

1 tablespoon (15 ml) extra virgin olive oil

½ yellow onion, finely chopped

2 cloves garlic, minced

1 teaspoon ground black pepper

1½ tablespoons (21 g) salted butter

5¼ ounces (150 g) mushrooms, thinly sliced

¾ cup (180 ml) heavy cream

2 teaspoons (10 ml) soy sauce

½ cup (50 g) finely grated Parmesan cheese, plus more for serving

Salt, to taste

Chopped fresh parsley leaves, for serving

Don't know what to make for dinner? Know this: A creamy pasta is always a safe choice! This pasta is as perfect as a weeknight dinner with the family as it is on the weekend together with a glass of red wine and your best friends. It is quick and easy, yet it still feels luxurious.

Instructions

Bring a pot of salted water to boil, and cook the pasta according to box instructions. Before draining, reserve 3 tablespoons (45 ml) of the pasta water, and set aside.

Meanwhile, in a large pan with high sides over medium heat, add the olive oil. Add the onion and cook until soft, about 2 minutes, stirring occasionally. Add the garlic and pepper and cook, stirring, for another minute.

Make a little hole in the center of the pan, and add the butter. When the butter is melted, add the mushrooms and cook, stirring occasionally, for 3 to 4 minutes or until the mushrooms are soft.

Pour the heavy cream into the pan, mix everything and let the cream heat through for a minute.

Add the soy sauce, pasta water and Parmesan, and mix everything until combined and creamy. Add salt to taste, and let the sauce simmer for a few minutes until thickened.

Pour the drained pasta into the sauce, add some fresh parsley to your liking and toss everything to combine.

Divide the pasta among two plates, and top with grated Parmesan and parsley.

CREAMY TOMATO AND BASIL PASTA

Prep: 10 min
Cook: 15 min
Total: 25 min
Servings: 2

Ingredients

6 ounces (170 g) short-shaped pasta (such as conchiglie, farfalle or fusilli)

1 tablespoon (15 ml) extra virgin olive oil

14 small cherry tomatoes, halved

1 large clove garlic, minced

4 ounces (115 g) cream cheese

½ cup (120 ml) heavy cream

2 tablespoons (7 g) chopped sun-dried tomatoes

1 teaspoon oil from the sun-dried tomatoes

1 teaspoon dried basil

½ teaspoon ground black pepper

½ vegetable bouillon cube

1 cup (30 g) baby spinach

Mini mozzarella balls, for serving

This recipe is very special to me because it was the first pasta dish to go viral on my TikTok account. Today, this video has been viewed by millions of people all over the world. I've made some adjustments since I first created this dish, and I can tell you that today this is still one of my favorite pasta dishes. Why? It's so simple yet packed with flavor. The creaminess of the sauce and cheesy mozzarella makes it just perfect. You can make it for yourself at lunch or invite your family and friends over for dinner. This recipe fits every occasion.

If you would like some extra protein with your pasta, add 10 ounces (283 g) of chicken breast (diced and cooked separately before adding into the sauce).

Instructions

Bring a pot of salted water to boil, and cook the pasta according to box instructions. Before draining, reserve 2 tablespoons (30 ml) of the pasta water, and set aside.

Meanwhile, heat the olive oil in a large frying pan over medium heat. Add the tomatoes, and cook until soft, about 5 minutes. Add the garlic, and use a spatula to mash the tomatoes and their juices with the garlic.

Add the cream cheese, heavy cream, sun-dried tomatoes, sun-dried tomato oil, dried basil, pepper and the bouillon, and mix until combined. Make sure the bouillon dissolves. Add the spinach, and let it soften while stirring, about 1 minute.

Pour the drained pasta into the sauce and toss. Top the pasta with mini mozzarella balls to taste.

LEMON AND CREAM CHEESE SALMON PASTA

Ingredients

12 ounces (340 g) linguine

2 tablespoons (28 g) salted butter (¼ stick)

2 large cloves garlic, minced

½ cup (120 ml) white wine (cooking wine is fine)

7 ounces (200 g) cream cheese

6½ tablespoons (100 ml) heavy cream

1 teaspoon dried thyme

Zest of 1 lemon

2 tablespoons (30 ml) lemon juice (from ½ lemon)

¼ teaspoon salt, plus more to taste

¾ teaspoon ground black pepper, plus more to taste

18 ounces (500 g) salmon, diced

2 cups (60 g) baby spinach

Salmon meets garlic, lemon and white wine in this pasta dish. The sauce has the perfect balance between acidity and buttery creaminess. This is a great weeknight dinner to make in under 30 minutes, and cooking the salmon in the sauce takes away a lot of effort. My family loves this dish, and I'm sure your family will, too.

Instructions

Bring a pot of salted water to boil, and cook the pasta according to box instructions. Before draining, reserve 3 tablespoons (45 ml) of the pasta water, and set aside.

In a large pan with high sides over medium heat, add the butter. Once the butter starts to sizzle, add the garlic and cook, stirring, for about 30 seconds. Add the white wine, and let it simmer for 5 minutes, stirring occasionally.

Add the cream cheese and heavy cream, and stir until the cream cheese is melted, about 1 minute. Add the thyme, and reduce the heat to low.

Add the lemon zest and juice to the sauce.

Add the salt, pepper and reserved pasta water, and stir to combine.

Increase the heat to medium, add the salmon, and make sure it's covered with the sauce. When the sauce is simmering, let the salmon continue to cook in the sauce until cooked through, about 5 minutes.

Add the spinach, and cook until softened, about 1 minute. Add the drained pasta to the sauce, and toss.

CREAMY BACON AND BROCCOLI PASTA

Prep: 5 min
Cook: 20 min
Total: 25 min
Servings: 4

Ingredients

8½ ounces (240 g) frozen broccoli florets

12 ounces (340 g) short-shaped pasta (such as fusilli, farfalle or penne)

7 ounces (200 g) bacon, chopped

1 small yellow onion, finely chopped

7 ounces (200 g) cream cheese

¾ cup (180 ml) heavy cream

1 beef bouillon cube

¼ teaspoon cayenne pepper, plus more to taste

I don't know who loves this pasta more, me or the kids I used to babysit. It's definitely a favorite among all ages, and it's a great way to get kids to eat broccoli. This is a perfect weeknight dinner with few ingredients that's easy to make. By using frozen broccoli, there's not much to prepare. But if you do want to add something extra, serve this with my homemade garlic bread (page 126).

Instructions

Place the frozen broccoli in a bowl, and cover it with hot water. Let the broccoli sit until it is defrosted, about 3 minutes.

Bring a pot of salted water to boil, and cook the pasta according to box instructions. Before draining, reserve ¼ cup (60 ml) of the pasta water, and set aside.

Heat a large pan with high sides over high heat, and add the bacon. When the bacon starts to sizzle, reduce the heat to medium-high, and continue cooking the bacon until it starts to get crispy, 3 to 4 minutes.

Reduce the heat to medium. Add the onion, and cook, stirring, until softened, about 2 minutes.

Add the cream cheese and heavy cream, and stir until the cream cheese is melted, about 1 minute. Then add the reserved pasta water, bouillon cube and cayenne pepper. Stir to make sure the bouillon cube dissolves.

Reduce the heat a little, and let the sauce simmer while preparing the broccoli. Drain the broccoli florets, and place them on a cutting board. Cut the broccoli into bite-sized pieces.

Add the broccoli to the sauce, and let it simmer for 3 to 4 minutes or until the broccoli has softened but still has texture.

Pour the drained pasta into the sauce, toss and serve.

TWISTED ALFREDO PASTA WITH CRISPY CHICKEN

Prep: 10 min
Cook: 20 min
Total: 30 min
Servings: 2

Chicken
1 (8-ounce [226-g]) boneless, skinless chicken breast

¼ teaspoon salt

1 teaspoon garlic powder

¾ teaspoon ground black pepper

½ teaspoon paprika

¼ cup (14 g) panko bread crumbs

¼ cup (25 g) finely grated Parmesan cheese

1 egg, beaten

Pasta
6 ounces (170 g) fettuccine

4 tablespoons (55 g) salted butter (½ stick)

2 large cloves garlic, minced

1¼ cups (300 ml) heavy cream

1½ cups (150 g) grated Parmesan cheese

½ teaspoon salt

½ teaspoon ground black pepper, plus more to taste

Fresh parsley leaves, for garnish

Note: If you only find 2 smaller chicken filets (about 4 ounces [150 g] each), you can put them in a plastic bag, and use any heavy flat object to flatten them to the right thickness.

When I moved to the United States in 2010 to work as an au pair for a year, I met some new friends. During my second week, they took me to The Cheesecake Factory, where I tried fettucine Alfredo for the very first time, and I fell in love with it. Back in Sweden, I knew I had to make it myself, and since I've always been a big fan of breaded chicken, I thought it would be a great addition, so I created this Alfredo recipe with a twist.

Instructions
Place the chicken on a cutting board. Use one hand to press it down while you cut horizontally all the way through the chicken to get 2 evenly thick filets (about ½ inch [1 cm]).

In a small bowl, mix the salt, garlic powder, pepper and paprika together. Spread the spice mixture all over the chicken until the spices cover both sides of the filets.

On a small plate, mix the panko and Parmesan. Place the beaten egg in a shallow bowl. Dip both chicken filets in the beaten egg, then the panko mixture. Spray both sides of the chicken with cooking spray. Place the chicken in the air fryer, and cook on 355°F [180°C] for 14 to 15 minutes (or in an oven preheated to 355°F [180°C]).

While the chicken breasts are cooking, bring a pot of salted water to boil, and cook the pasta according to box instructions.

In a medium-sized pan with high sides, place the butter, and heat over medium heat. Once the butter starts to sizzle, add the garlic, and cook, stirring, for about 1 minute. Add the heavy cream, and allow it to heat through. Add the Parmesan, salt and pepper. Mix until well combined.

Toss the drained pasta with the sauce, and divide it between two plates. Add more black pepper to taste, and top each plate with 1 crispy chicken filet. Garnish with the fresh parsley.

TOMATO AND BURRATA PASTA

Prep: 5 min
Cook: 25 min
Total: 30 min
Servings: 4

Ingredients
3 tablespoons (45 ml) extra virgin olive oil, plus more for serving

7 tablespoons (70 g) finely chopped shallot (about 2 whole)

2 large cloves garlic, finely chopped

½ teaspoon chili flakes

2 tablespoons (30 ml) tomato paste

1 (21-ounce [600-g]) can crushed tomatoes

½ teaspoon sugar

¾ teaspoon salt

½ teaspoon ground black pepper, plus more for serving

12 ounces (340 g) spaghetti

2½ tablespoons (8 g) finely chopped fresh basil leaves, divided

2 large (4-ounce [115-g]) balls of burrata cheese (see Note)

I always have canned tomatoes in my pantry, because you can make so many different dishes with them and they are very shelf-stable. This pasta is one of my favorites to make for lunch. It's both quick and simple to make with few ingredients. The creamy burrata definitely takes it to another level. When buying the canned tomatoes, always chose a high-quality brand; I think they taste so much better.

Instructions
In a large pan with high sides over medium-low heat, place the olive oil. Add the shallot, and cook, stirring, until soft, about 2 minutes. Add the garlic and chili flakes, and cook for about 30 seconds.

Reduce the heat to low, add the tomato paste, and cook, stirring occasionally, until it is dark brown and caramelized, about 4 minutes.

Pour the crushed tomatoes into the pan, and add the sugar, salt and pepper. Increase the heat to medium, and let the mixture simmer for about 10 minutes, stirring occasionally.

Meanwhile, bring a pot of salted water to boil, and cook the pasta according to box instructions. Before draining, reserve ¼ cup (60 ml) of the pasta water.

Add the pasta water to the crushed tomatoes with 2 tablespoons (7 g) of the freshly chopped basil. Mix until combined. Add the drained spaghetti and toss.

Serve the pasta from the pan, or transfer it to a large, shallow plate. Top the pasta with the burrata, using two forks to pull them apart. Drizzle some olive oil and sprinkle some black pepper on top of the burrata. Garnish with the remaining basil.

Note: If you can't find burrata at your grocery store, you can use fresh mini mozzarella balls instead.

CREAMY AVOCADO PASTA

Prep: 5 min
Cook: 15 min
Total: 20 min
Servings: 2

Pasta
6 ounces (170 g) penne

Avocado Sauce
1 cup (24 g) fresh basil leaves, plus more for garnish

½ cup (50 g) finely grated Parmesan cheese, plus more for garnish

1 clove garlic, peeled

⅛ teaspoon salt

½ teaspoon ground black pepper

½ tablespoon (8 ml) lemon juice

2 avocados, skin and pits removed

¼ cup (60 ml) extra virgin olive oil

If you love avocados as much as I do, you will love this pasta. This is a twist on my pesto pasta with flavors from basil, Parmesan and garlic. It's creamy, filling and crazy delicious. We all know how hard it is to find the perfect avocados, and if you have some that are about to go bad, this is a great way to use them.

Instructions
Bring a pot of salted water to boil, and cook the pasta according to box instructions. Before draining, reserve 2 tablespoons (30 ml) of the pasta water.

Meanwhile in a blender or a food processor, add the basil, Parmesan, garlic, salt, pepper, lemon juice and avocados, and blend on high speed until combined, 15 to 30 seconds.

Reduce the speed to low. Slowly add the olive oil to the avocado mixture. Turn the blender off as soon as you've added all the olive oil (blending the olive oil too fast or for too long will make the sauce taste bitter). If you don't have a blender or a food processor, you can blend by hand using a mortar and pestle.

Add the sauce and the pasta water to a large bowl, then add the drained pasta and toss. Garnish with Parmesan and basil.

Note: Serve this pasta with some toasted pine nuts for texture.

SIMPLE CHICKEN CURRY PASTA

Prep: 5 min
Cook: 15 min
Total: 20 min
Servings: 4

Ingredients

10 ounces (280 g) short-shaped pasta (such as fusilli, farfalle or penne)

1 tablespoon (14 g) salted butter

14 ounces (390 g) chicken breast, cut into 1-inch cubes

½ teaspoon ground black pepper

1½ cups (360 ml) heavy cream

1 tablespoon (15 ml) chicken broth

1 tablespoon (6 g) yellow curry powder

1 teaspoon onion powder

1½ tablespoons (22.5 g) light brown sugar

1 cup (100 g) finely grated Parmesan cheese

Fresh arugula, for serving

Pasta done in 20 minutes? Yes, please! The word *curry* refers to a spiced sauce. I don't know why, but I always crave this pasta in the winter. Maybe it's something about the curry that's warming on a cold day. Or maybe it's because I usually travel to Asia for vacation during the winter, where curry is very common. Either way, this dish is delicious.

Instructions

Bring a pot of salted water to boil, and cook the pasta according to box instructions. Before draining, reserve ¼ cup (60 ml) of the pasta water.

In a large pan with high sides over medium-high heat, add the butter. Once the butter starts to sizzle, add the chicken and pepper, and cook until the chicken is cooked through, about 5 minutes.

Reduce the heat to medium. Add the heavy cream, chicken broth, curry powder, onion powder and brown sugar, and stir to coat the chicken.

Add the pasta water and Parmesan. Stir until the cheese is melted, then reduce the heat to low, and let the sauce simmer, stirring occasionally, for about 3 minutes or until it has thickened.

Add the drained pasta and toss. Serve with fresh arugula on top.

Note: Not a fan of Parmesan? Leave it out, and replace half of the heavy cream with cream cheese; this will make the sauce creamy without the Parmesan.

FOR LAZY DAYS

Impressive recipes don't have to take hours to make. We all have those stressful weeknights when we're busy with other commitments and tired from a long day. In the same time it would take you to go get some fast food, you can cook these homemade meals. This book is all about simple food, but can it get even simpler? The answer is yes! In this chapter, I've gathered my easiest recipes for extremely lazy days. These recipes call for simple ingredients and even fewer steps that require minimal effort. There's little to no preparation needed, and very little cleanup afterward, leaving time for you to relax.

GARLIC MAC AND CHEESE WITH DOUBLE CHEESE AND CRISPY BACON CRUMBLES

Ingredients

12 ounces (340 g) elbow macaroni

8 slices bacon, chopped

½ cup (115 g) salted butter (1 stick)

2 cloves garlic, minced

4 tablespoons (32 g) whole wheat flour

1½ cups (360 ml) low-fat milk

1 teaspoon paprika

½ teaspoon salt

2½ teaspoons (6 g) white pepper

2 cups (224 g) shredded Cheddar cheese

2 cups (200 g) freshly grated Parmesan cheese

Mac and cheese is a classic favorite made for the whole family. The sharp flavor from the Parmesan and garlic will impress the adults. And don't worry, we've kept the classic Cheddar cheese for those still dreaming about their childhood.

Instructions

Bring a pot of salted water to boil, and cook the pasta according to box instructions.

In a large pan, place the bacon, and heat it over high heat. When the bacon starts to sizzle, reduce the heat to medium-high, and continue to cook until the bacon is crispy, 3 to 4 minutes. Remove the bacon from the pan, and place it on a paper towel to drain.

In a large pot over medium heat, place the butter. Once the butter starts to sizzle, add the garlic. Cook, whisking, for about 30 seconds. Keep whisking while adding the flour.

Once the flour is mixed in, reduce the heat to medium-low. Add the milk, paprika, salt and white pepper to the pot, and whisk until combined.

Add the Cheddar and Parmesan, and stir until the cheese is melted, about 1 minute.

Remove the cheese sauce from the heat, and pour the drained macaroni into it. Toss until all the macaroni is covered in the sauce.

Divide the mac and cheese among four shallow plates, and top each plate with a quarter of the crispy bacon crumbles.

PIZZA ROLLS

Prep: 5 min
Cook: 20 to 25 min
Total: 25 to 30 min
Servings: 14 to 16 rolls

Pizza Sauce
(Makes ⅓ cup [80 ml])
5 tablespoons (75 ml) canned finely crushed tomatoes

2 tablespoons (30 ml) tomato paste

½ tablespoon (1 g) dried oregano

¼ teaspoon salt

Pizza Rolls
All-purpose flour, for dusting

1 premade rectangular pizza crust (about 12 x 14 inch [30 x 35 cm] long and ¼ inch [0.5 cm] thick)

⅓ cup (80 ml) pizza sauce

1 cup (112 g) finely shredded mozzarella cheese

2 slices smoked deli ham, diced

I loved these when I was a kid and still do. By making a very simple, quick and delicious pizza sauce at home and using a premade pizza crust, these rolls are done in no time. This is a great activity to do with your kids, so why not let them be a part of the cooking process? When I was little, I loved making these as much as I loved eating them.

Instructions
Preheat the oven according to the pizza crust package instructions.

In a medium bowl, combine the crushed tomatoes, tomato paste, oregano and salt, and stir until incorporated. Set aside.

Flour a clean, flat work surface. Use a rolling pin to roll out the pizza crust on the floured surface.

Spread the pizza sauce over the pizza crust. Top the pizza sauce with the mozzarella cheese and the ham.

Starting at one of the longer sides, roll the pizza crust so the filling is on the inside. Pinch the pizza crust where it ends to close it up.

Cut the pizza into small rolls (about 1 inch [2.5 cm] thick).

Place parchment paper on a baking sheet, and add the pizza rolls, leaving some space in between each roll. Bake the rolls according to the crust package instructions, about 10 minutes.

HEALTHY BANANA PANCAKES

Prep: 0 min
Cook: 10 to 15 min
Total: 10 to 15 min
Servings: 2 to 3 (about 15 thin pancakes)

Ingredients
2 bananas

4 eggs

1 teaspoon vanilla extract

¼ teaspoon salt

2 tablespoons (30 ml) canola oil, plus more for frying

Fresh berries, for serving

Maple syrup, for serving

Are you someone like me who would love to have pancakes for breakfast every day? With this recipe, you can! These pancakes are not only nutritious but so tasty and quick to make. And if you have a picky toddler, this will save your day! Try substituting cinnamon for the vanilla extract if you'd prefer another flavor.

Instructions
In a large bowl, add the bananas, eggs, vanilla, salt and canola oil, and use a handheld mixer or blender to mix until combined and smooth, about 30 seconds. You can also mix this by hand by using a whisk; just mash the bananas before whisking.

Heat a large pan over medium-low heat, and brush some canola oil on the pan. Pour about ¼ cup (60 ml) of the batter into the pan for each pancake, making 3 to 4 at a time. Cook the pancakes on both sides, 2 to 3 minutes total, and serve with fresh berries and maple syrup.

Note: If you want to make them more filling, add ½ cup (45 g) instant oats. This will also add healthy carbohydrates.

SPICY CHORIZO PASTA

Prep: 5 min
Cook: 15 min
Total: 20 min
Servings: 4

Ingredients

10 ounces (280 g) spaghetti

8 egg yolks

1 cup (100 g) finely grated Pecorino or Parmesan cheese

7 ounces (200 g) chorizo, diced

½ teaspoon salt

½ teaspoon ground black pepper

Chili flakes, for serving

This recipe is similar to a carbonara, and originally I called it "chorizo carbonara," but as always I like to change things up a bit. If you've ever had carbonara, you'll still recognize the flavors from the eggs and Parmesan, but with the spicy chorizo, this pasta is something else.

Instructions

Bring a pot of salted water to boil, and cook the pasta according to box instructions. Before draining, reserve 3 tablespoons (45 ml) of the pasta water.

In a medium-sized bowl, add the egg yolks and beat them with a fork. Then add the cheese, and stir to combine.

In a large pan over high heat, add the chorizo. Once the chorizo starts to sizzle, reduce the heat to medium, and cook for about 3 minutes or until the chorizo is heated through and has formed a crust.

While whisking, add the pasta water to the egg mixture until the cheese starts to melt and the mixture has a smooth consistency.

Reduce the heat to low, and add the drained pasta to the chorizo, followed by the egg mixture, tossing to combine. Once the cheese has melted, remove the pan from the heat to prevent the eggs from overcooking.

Add the salt and black pepper, toss again, and plate. Garnish with sprinkles of chili flakes to taste.

SIMPLE TOMATO SOUP

Prep: 5 min
Cook: 20 min
Total: 25 min
Servings: 2 to 3

Ingredients

2 tablespoons (30 ml) extra virgin olive oil

1 small yellow onion, diced

1 large clove garlic, chopped

1 (28-ounce [794-g]) can crushed tomatoes

1½ teaspoons (6 g) sugar

1½ teaspoons (1 g) dried oregano

½ teaspoon salt

½ teaspoon ground black pepper

1 vegetable bouillon cube

½ cup (120 ml) heavy cream

This is a very easy and delicious creamy soup with a pretty color. It's perfect if you're having dinner late in the evening and don't want something that's too heavy. Serve it warm in the fall or cold in the summer.

Instructions

In a medium-sized pot over medium-low heat, add the olive oil. Add the onion, and cook for about 2 minutes, stirring occasionally. Add the garlic, and cook for another minute.

Pour the crushed tomatoes into the pot, and add the sugar, oregano, salt and pepper. Increase the heat to medium, partially cover the pot with a lid and allow the tomatoes to simmer for about 10 minutes.

Add the bouillon cube, stirring to make sure it dissolves. Add the heavy cream. Once the cream is heated through, remove the pot from the heat.

Use a handheld blender to blend the soup until smooth, about 1 minute. (You can also use a stationary blender; just make sure it's heat resistant.)

Note: I like to serve this soup with my grilled cheese sandwich (page 61).

EXTRA-CHEESY GRILLED CHEESE

Prep: 5 min
Cook: 10 min
Total: 15 min
Servings: 2

Ingredients

4 slices white bread

Salted butter

2 slices Cheddar cheese

½ cup (50 g) finely grated Parmesan cheese

2 slices Pepper Jack cheese

Mayonnaise

Grilled cheese is a classic American sandwich that has been around for ages. Eat it by itself or as a side to my creamy tomato soup (page 58). When it comes to the cheese, you can use any type you like, so feel free to mix it up! I prefer to mix Cheddar, Pepper Jack and Parmesan for a slightly sharper taste than with the classic American cheese. The best grilled cheese is crunchy on the outside and a real mess on the inside.

Instructions

Spread one side of each slice of bread with butter.

Layer a slice of buttered bread (buttered side facing out) with 1 slice of Cheddar, half of the Parmesan and 1 slice of Pepper Jack. Repeat with another piece of buttered bread and the remaining cheese.

Top each sandwich with another piece of buttered bread, butter side facing the cheese. Use your hand to press down the sandwiches a little.

Heat a large pan over medium heat. Spread mayonnaise all over the top slice of the two sandwiches, and place them in the pan with the mayonnaise side down.

Spread mayonnaise over the slices of bread facing up. Cook for 2 minutes, or until the bottoms are golden brown. Flip the sandwiches, reduce the heat a little, and add a tiny splash of water to the side of the pan, putting a lid over the pan to create steam. This will melt the cheese inside the sandwiches.

Cook until the cheese is melted and the bread is golden brown, about 2 minutes more.

Note: Want to spice up your grilled cheese? Try adding caramelized onions, garlic or bacon.

LEMON AND RICOTTA CHICKEN PASTA

Prep: 5 to 10 min
Cook: 15 min
Total: 20 to 25 min
Servings: 4

Ingredients
12 ounces (340 g) spaghetti

3 tablespoons (45 ml) extra virgin olive oil

14 ounces (390 g) boneless, skinless chicken breast, diced

1 teaspoon salt, plus more to taste

1 teaspoon ground black pepper, plus more for serving

2 cloves garlic, minced

18 ounces (550 g) whole-milk ricotta cheese

Zest of 1 lemon

¼ cup (60 ml) lemon juice (about 1 large lemon)

2½ cups (75 g) baby spinach

This super simple pasta is bursting with flavor. It's high in acidity, but the mild and creamy ricotta provides the perfect balance. You'll make this pasta in no time. The cleanup will be minimal, so you can sit back after eating and relax.

Instructions
Bring a pot of salted water to boil, and cook the pasta according to box instructions. Before draining, reserve ½ cup (120 ml) of the pasta water.

In a large pan with high sides over medium-high heat, add the olive oil.

Add the chicken, salt and pepper to the pan. Cook until the chicken is almost cooked through, about 4 minutes. Reduce the heat to medium-low, add the garlic, and cook, stirring, for another minute.

Add the ricotta, lemon zest and juice and pasta water. Stir until everything is mixed. Add the spinach, and cook until soft, about 1 minute. Add more salt to taste.

Add the drained pasta, toss and serve with some black pepper on top.

PIZZADILLAS

Prep: 5 to 10 min
Cook: 20 min
Total: 25 to 30 min
Servings: 4

Ingredients

4 large flour tortillas

⅔ cup (160 ml) pizza sauce (page 53), divided

2 cups (224 g) finely shredded mozzarella cheese

Pepperoni, thinly sliced

Red onion, sliced

Green bell peppers, sliced

This recipe is a mix between a pizza and a quesadilla. I love them both, so it's no surprise that this has become my new go-to meal when I don't know what to cook and don't want to go to the grocery store. I usually have everything at home, and since you can make this with so many different ingredients, it's a great way to empty your refrigerator. The whole family can choose their own favorite toppings. It's such a fun and easy thing to make together, so you can get some quality family time while cooking.

Instructions

Place 2 tortillas on a clean, flat surface, and spread each with half of the pizza sauce. Make sure the whole tortilla is covered.

Heat two large pans over medium-low heat. Gently place the tortillas in separate pans with the sauce facing up.

Add ½ cup (56 g) of the mozzarella on top of each pizza. Add the pepperoni, onion and bell peppers. Spread the toppings evenly over each pizza.

Add another ½ cup (56 g) of mozzarella on top of each pizza. Then spread the remaining pizza sauce on each of the remaining tortillas, and place them sauce side down on top of the pizzas. Use your hand or a spatula to press them down.

Cook until the bottoms of the tortillas are golden brown, about 5 minutes. Carefully flip, and cook for about 3 minutes on the other side.

Remove the pizzas from the pan, and cut each in half, one half per person. Cut each half into two to four slices, and serve.

SANDWICHES AND BURGERS

If someone asks me for a go-to meal, I give them one of these recipes. Because who can say no to a sandwich packed with flavor or a juicy burger? The sandwiches are perfect for a weekend breakfast, a quick lunch or an evening snack, and I make a burger for dinner at least once a week. When it comes to sandwiches and burgers, I often say, "The greasier the better," but I've also shared one of my favorite low-carb recipes, a Chaffle BLT (page 71). This chapter has something for everyone.

GRILLED PESTO AND MOZZARELLA SANDWICH

Prep: 10 min
Cook: 15 min
Total: 25 min
Servings: 2

Ingredients

½ cup (120 ml) pesto, plus more to taste (page 30)

4 slices sourdough bread (about 1 inch [2.5 cm] thick)

1 fresh mozzarella ball (about 4.5 ounces [125 g]), sliced

4 thin tomato slices

Flaky sea salt, to taste

Ground black pepper, to taste

Salted butter, softened

The first time I had a sandwich similar to this was at a small Swedish coffee shop, and I immediately went home to remake it. Not much beats this warm and toasty sandwich with lots of flavor and melted mozzarella. For this recipe, I use my homemade pesto, but if you're in a rush you can use store-bought. When I want to switch it up, I add some cream cheese and mashed avocado as well.

Instructions

Spread the pesto evenly on all 4 slices of bread. Divide the mozzarella between 2 of the bread slices.

Add 2 slices of tomato (side by side) on top of 2 slices of mozzarella (4 slices in total for the 2 sandwiches), and sprinkle the salt and black pepper to taste.

Put the slice of bread that's only spread with pesto on top of the tomato with the pesto facing down. Repeat with the other sandwich.

Heat a large frying pan over medium-low heat. Spread the butter on top of both sandwiches, and put them in the pan with the butter side down. Spread more butter on the other side of the bread. Cook until the bread facing the pan is golden brown, about 3 minutes, then flip the sandwiches. Reduce the heat, and add a tiny splash of water to the pan. Put a lid over the pan to create steam. This will melt the mozzarella inside the sandwich.

Cook until the mozzarella is melted and the other slice of bread is golden brown, about 2 minutes. Remove the sandwiches, and serve.

Note: You can make the sandwiches in a panini press instead of using a frying pan.

CHAFFLE BLT

Prep: 10 min
Cook: 15 to 20 min
Total: 25 to 30 min
Servings: 2

Chaffle Batter
4 eggs
2½ cups (280 g) finely shredded mozzarella cheese
½ teaspoon salt

BLT
6 slices bacon
4 chaffles
Mayonnaise
1 cup (47 g) shredded lettuce
4 tomato slices
Salt, to taste
Ground black pepper, to taste

The word *chaffle* refers to a waffle made out of cheese and egg. In my sandwich, the chaffles will replace the bread, making this a low-carb recipe. But that doesn't mean it's low on flavor. This recipe calls for the same ingredients as a regular BLT with a more flavorful "bread." This is my mom's favorite, and she asks me to make it for her every time she comes over. And who am I to say no when it's so simple?

Instructions
Preheat a waffle iron to high.

Make the chaffle batter. In a medium-sized bowl, whisk together the eggs, mozzarella and salt. Pour a quarter of the batter into the hot waffle iron. Cook until golden brown, 3 to 4 minutes. Repeat with the remaining batter.

Meanwhile, in a large pan, place the bacon, and heat it over high heat. When the bacon starts to sizzle, reduce the heat to medium-high, and cook until the bacon is crispy, 3 to 4 minutes. Remove the bacon from the pan, and place it on a paper towel or a rack to drain.

Once the chaffles are done, place 2 of the chaffles on separate plates, and spread them both with mayonnaise. Add half of the bacon to each chaffle, followed by half of the lettuce and 2 slices of tomato.

Sprinkle some salt and black pepper to taste on the tomatoes. Spread the rest of the mayonnaise on the 2 remaining chaffles, and place them on top of the tomatoes, mayonnaise side down.

Note: If you are making the chaffles one at a time, place them in a preheated oven (about 215°F [100°C]) to keep them warm while making the rest.

HONEY-LIME CHICKEN BURGER

Prep: 10 min
Cook: 20 min
Total: 30 min
Servings: 2

Chicken

1 (8-ounce [226-g]) boneless, skinless chicken breast (see Note)

½ teaspoon salt

1 teaspoon garlic powder

¾ teaspoon ground black pepper

½ teaspoon paprika

½ cup (28 g) panko bread crumbs

1 egg, beaten

Burger

½ tablespoon (8 ml) extra virgin olive oil, divided

2 potato or brioche hamburger buns

8 pickle slices

2 lettuce leaves

Honey-Lime Marinade (page 118)

1 cup (200 g) coleslaw (store-bought or homemade [page 76])

You'd think that the star of this burger is the crispy chicken breast, but it's actually my Honey-Lime Marinade (page 118). This marinade has become my new obsession, and there's no way to put into words how good it is. You have to try it for yourself to understand what I mean.

Instructions

Place the chicken on a cutting board. Use one hand to press it down while you cut horizontally all the way through the chicken to get 2 evenly thick filets (about ½ inch [1 cm]).

In a small bowl, mix the salt, garlic powder, pepper and paprika together. Spread the spice mixture all over the chicken until the spices cover both sides of the filets.

Place the panko on a small plate. Place the beaten egg in a shallow bowl.

Dip both chicken filets in the beaten egg, then the panko. Spray both sides of the chicken with cooking spray. Place the chicken in the air fryer, and cook on 355°F (180°C) for 14 to 15 minutes (or in an oven preheated to 355°F [180°C]).

When the chicken has about 4 minutes left, add the olive oil to a large pan and heat over medium heat. Place the hamburger buns in the pan cut side down, and cook until golden brown, about 2 minutes.

Place the 2 bottom buns on two separate plates. Divide the pickles between the buns, followed by 1 lettuce leaf.

Add 1 chicken filet to each burger, and drizzle the Honey-Lime Marinade all over the crispy chicken. Add half of the coleslaw to each burger and finish with the top buns, and serve immediately.

Note: If you only find 2 smaller chicken filets (about 4 ounces [150 g] each), you can put them in a plastic bag, and use any heavy flat object to flatten them to the right thickness.

AVOCADO MELT WITH JALAPEÑO SPREAD

Prep: 5 min
Cook: 15 min
Total: 20 min
Servings: 2

Jalapeño Spread
(makes 4 tablespoons [60 ml])
2½ ounces (75 g) cream cheese

3 tablespoons (30 g) finely chopped pickled jalapeños

⅛ teaspoon salt

½ teaspoon ground black pepper

Sandwiches
4 slices sourdough bread (about ½ inch [1 cm] thick)

4 slices Cheddar cheese

1 avocado, mashed

Salted butter, softened

This is my favorite meatless sandwich. The creamy avocado and sharp cheese go so well with the spicy jalapeño spread. And who can resist a buttered, crispy slice of sourdough? For all this simplicity, there's so much flavor that you don't need to add anything else. It's as good for breakfast as it is for lunch or a late-night snack. And oh, I forgot to tell you the best part...it's super easy to make!

Instructions

Make the Jalapeño Spread. In a small bowl, add the cream cheese, pickled jalapeños, salt and pepper, and stir to combine.

Spread a quarter of the Jalapeño Spread on a slice of sourdough, then add a slice of Cheddar cheese on top.

Add half of the mashed avocado on top of the cheese, followed by another slice of cheese. Repeat with another piece of bread.

Take the 2 remaining slices of bread, and spread one side with Jalapeño Spread. Place them on top of the Cheddar cheese as a lid for the sandwiches with the Jalapeño Spread facing the cheese.

Heat a large pan over medium heat. Spread butter on top of the 2 sandwiches, and put them in the pan buttered side down. Spread butter on the tops of the bread. Cook until the bottoms are golden brown, about 2 minutes. Flip the sandwiches, reduce the heat, and add a tiny splash of water to the side of the pan. Cover the pan with a lid to create steam, and cook for another 2 minutes until the cheese is melted.

Note: You can also grill the sandwiches in a panini press, but be careful not to press them down too hard because the mashed avocado will squeeze out.

CRISPY CHICKEN BURGER

Prep: 10 min
Cook: 20 min
Total: 30 min
Servings: 2

Chicken
1 (8-ounce [226-g]) boneless, skinless chicken breast (see Note)

½ teaspoon salt

1 teaspoon garlic powder

¾ teaspoon ground black pepper

½ teaspoon paprika

½ cup (28 g) panko bread crumbs

1 egg, beaten

Red Coleslaw
1½ cups (75 g) finely shredded red cabbage

1½ tablespoons (23 ml) mayonnaise

2½ tablespoons (38 ml) sour cream

1 teaspoon Dijon mustard

1 teaspoon apple cider vinegar

¼ teaspoon salt

½ teaspoon ground black pepper

½ teaspoon sugar

Even though I love a juicy beef burger, crispy chicken burgers are my favorite. I always thought breading chicken at home would be such hard work, but it's actually really simple. I've made it even easier by not frying them in a pan, because I've realized they're just as good made in the air fryer or the oven. I add my homemade red coleslaw to this burger together with chili mayonnaise. I promise you it's so much better than takeout.

Instructions

Place the chicken on a cutting board. Use one hand to press it down while you cut horizontally all the way through the chicken to get 2 evenly thick filets (about ½ inch [1 cm]).

In a small bowl, mix the salt, garlic powder, pepper and paprika together. Spread the spice mixture all over the chicken until the spices cover both sides of the filets.

Place the panko on a small plate. Place the beaten egg in a shallow bowl.

Dip both chicken filets in the beaten egg, then the panko. Spray both sides of the chicken with cooking spray. Place the chicken in the air fryer, and cook on 355°F (180°C) for 14 to 15 minutes (or in an oven preheated to 355°F [180°C]).

While the chicken is cooking, make the coleslaw. In a medium-sized bowl, add the cabbage, mayonnaise, sour cream, Dijon mustard, vinegar, salt, pepper and sugar, and stir to combine. Refrigerate the coleslaw until ready to use.

Burgers

4 tablespoons (60 ml) mayonnaise

1½ tablespoons (23 ml) chili sauce (or you can substitute 1½ tablespoons [23 ml] ketchup and add ¼ teaspoon chili powder)

½ tablespoon (8 ml) extra virgin olive oil

2 brioche hamburger buns

1 tablespoon (10 g) thinly sliced red onion

2 lettuce leaves

4 thin tomato slices

In a small bowl, combine the mayonnaise and chili sauce.

When the chicken has about 4 minutes left, in a large pan over medium heat, place the olive oil. Place the burger buns in the pan cut side down, and cook until golden brown, about 2 minutes.

Build your burgers. Place half of the chili mayonnaise on each bottom bun, then add half the red onion, 1 piece chicken, half the lettuce, half the tomato and half the coleslaw. Place the top buns over the burgers, and serve.

Note: If you only find 2 smaller chicken filets (about 4 ounces [150 g] each), you can put them in a plastic bag, and use any heavy flat object to flatten them to the right thickness.

SPICY TUNA MELT

Prep: 10 min
Cook: 15 min
Total: 25 min
Servings: 4

Tuna Filling

12 ounces (340 g) canned tuna, drained

½ cup (120 ml) mayonnaise

2 teaspoons (10 ml) soy sauce

6 tablespoons (40 g) finely chopped red onion

1 cup (149 g) finely chopped tomato

½ teaspoon ground black pepper

3 tablespoons (45 ml) Sriracha

Sandwiches

8 slices sourdough bread (about ½ inch [1 cm] thick)

8 slices Cheddar cheese

4 tablespoons (55 g) salted butter, at room temperature

Chopped fresh parsley, for garnish (optional)

This spicy tuna melt is so good I can't stop making it. I'm going to be honest with you: I've never liked canned tuna. Even though I've tried it many times, I just couldn't understand why people were craving it until I made this sandwich for my fiancé. Of course I can't cook something without trying it, and I seriously ended up eating the whole thing myself. But I did make him a new one, and he loved it, too.

___

Instructions

Place the tuna in a small bowl or on a plate, and use a fork to break it into flakes.

In a large bowl, combine the mayonnaise, soy sauce, red onion, tomato, pepper and Sriracha, and mix well. Add in the tuna and mix well.

On a slice of bread, put 1 slice of Cheddar cheese. Add a quarter of the tuna filling and spread it out evenly.

Add another slice of Cheddar cheese on top of the tuna filling, followed by another slice of bread. Repeat with the remaining ingredients to make 4 sandwiches.

Heat two large pans over medium heat. Spread butter on the tops of the sandwiches, and put them in the pans, 2 sandwiches in each pan, buttered side down.

Spread butter on the other slices of bread, which are now facing up. Cook until golden brown, about 2 minutes. Flip the sandwiches, reduce the heat and add a tiny splash of water to the side of the pans. Cover the pans with lids, and cook until the cheese is melted, about 2 minutes.

Remove the sandwiches, cut them in half diagonally, garnish with parsley if using, and serve.

BIG MAC COPYCAT BURGER

Prep: 10 min
Cook: 20 min
Total: 30 min
Servings: 2

My Big Mac Dressing
(makes 4 tablespoons [60 ml])
3 tablespoons (45 ml) mayonnaise

½ tablespoon (8 ml) yellow mustard

1½ tablespoons (22 g) finely chopped pickles

1½ tablespoons (15 g) finely chopped yellow onion

¼ teaspoon white wine vinegar

½ teaspoon garlic powder

½ teaspoon paprika

Burgers
12 ounces (340 g) ground beef

2 tablespoons (30 ml) extra virgin olive oil, divided

Salt, to taste

Ground black pepper, to taste

4 slices Cheddar cheese

4 sesame seed hamburger buns, plus 2 hamburger bun bottoms

2 handfuls finely shredded lettuce

6 pickle slices

Do you love a Big Mac but are tired of fast food? Let's make it at home! This version is more nutritious and, in my opinion, tastier. This is a copycat burger, but I've made a few adjustments. Instead of placing the onions on the burger, I add them to the dressing. This keeps them from falling out and it also gives the dressing some extra flavor. The original Big Mac only has cheese on the bottom patty, but I've added cheese to both, because the more cheese the better, according to me.

Instructions

Make the dressing. In a small bowl, combine the mayonnaise, mustard, pickles, onion, vinegar, garlic powder and paprika. Refrigerate the dressing until ready to serve.

Divide the ground beef into quarters, and roll each quarter into a ball.

In a large pan, place 1 tablespoon (15 ml) of the olive oil, and heat over high heat.

Once the pan is hot, add the balls of beef, leaving room in between each. Use anything hard and flat (such as a burger press, spatula or the bottom of a pot) with some parchment paper in between to press the patties as flat as possible. Season the top side of each patty with salt and black pepper.

Cook the patties until the bottoms have a dark brown crust, about 2 minutes. Flip the patties, and cook for 2 minutes more. Remove the burgers from the pan, and immediately place a slice of cheese on top of each patty.

In the same pan, add the remaining 1 tablespoon (15 ml) of olive oil, and place the burger buns (tops and bottoms) cut side down. Cook until golden brown, about 2 minutes. Repeat with the extra bottom burger buns. Remove the toasted buns, and set aside.

Build your burgers in this order: bottom bun, 1 tablespoon (15 ml) of dressing, ½ handful of lettuce, 1 patty with cheese, bottom bun, 1 tablespoon (15 ml) of dressing, ½ handful of lettuce, 3 pickle slices, 1 patty with cheese and top bun.

SPICY SMASHBURGER

Prep: 5 min
Cook: 25 min
Total: 30 min
Servings: 2

**Sriracha Mayonnaise
(makes 4 tablespoons [60 ml])**
¼ cup (60 ml) mayonnaise

4 teaspoons (20 ml) Sriracha

½ teaspoon garlic powder

½ teaspoon sugar

Pinch of salt

Burgers
1½ tablespoons (21 g) salted butter

1 large yellow onion, thinly sliced

1 teaspoon sugar

4 slices bacon

11½ ounces (325 g) ground beef

Salt, to taste

Ground black pepper, to taste

2 slices Pepper Jack cheese

½ tablespoon (8 ml) extra virgin olive oil

2 hamburger buns

A smashburger is a ball of ground beef that is smashed down in a smoking-hot pan to create a thin, crispy and juicy burger patty. I make it even better by adding melted cheese in between each patty and topping it with sweet golden caramelized onions and salty bacon. Add some heat from the Sriracha, and you've got one of my favorite burgers!

Instructions

Make the Sriracha Mayonnaise. In a small bowl, combine the mayonnaise, Sriracha, garlic powder, sugar and salt. Set aside.

Heat a medium-sized pan over medium heat. Add the butter, onion and sugar. Reduce the heat to low, and cook, stirring occasionally, for about 10 minutes until the onion is caramelized and golden brown. Remove from the heat.

While the onion cooks, in a large pan, add the bacon, and heat it over high heat. When the bacon starts to sizzle, reduce the heat to medium-high, and cook until the bacon is crispy, 3 to 4 minutes. Remove the bacon from the pan, and place it on a paper towel or a rack to drain. Leave the bacon fat in the pan, and return the pan to the stove.

Divide the ground beef into quarters, and roll each quarter into a ball. Place the balls of beef in the pan with the bacon fat, leaving room between the balls. Use anything hard and flat (such as a burger press, spatula or the bottom of a pot) with some parchment paper in between, to press the patties as flat as possible. Season the tops of the patties with salt and black pepper.

Cook for about 2 minutes, or until the bottoms have formed a dark brown crust. Flip the patties, and cook for another 2 minutes. Remove the burgers from the pan, and immediately add a slice of Pepper Jack cheese to 2 of the patties. Place the remaining patties over the cheese, creating a double patty. Return the pan to the stove, and reduce the heat to medium. Add the olive oil, then add the burger buns cut side down. Cook until the buns are golden brown, about 2 minutes.

Build each burger in this order: bottom bun, 1 tablespoon (15 ml) of Sriracha mayonnaise, 1 double burger patty, 2 slices of bacon, half of the caramelized onion, 1 tablespoon (15 ml) of Sriracha mayonnaise and top bun.

AVOCADO-RANCH CHICKEN BURGER

Prep: 10 min
Cook: 20 min
Total: 30 min
Servings: 4

**Avocado-Ranch Dressing
(makes 1 cup [240 ml])**
½ cup (120 ml) sour cream

¼ cup (60 ml) buttermilk

¼ cup (60 ml) mayonnaise

½ teaspoon dried dill

1 large clove garlic

1 teaspoon freshly squeezed
lemon juice

1 avocado, skin and pit removed

1 tablespoon (3 g) finely chopped
fresh chives

¼ teaspoon salt

½ teaspoon ground black pepper

Chicken
2 (8-ounce [226-g]) boneless,
skinless chicken breasts

1 teaspoon salt

2 teaspoons (5 g) garlic powder

1½ teaspoons (3 g) ground black
pepper

1 teaspoon paprika

½ cup (56 g) panko bread crumbs

2 eggs, beaten

Burgers
1 tablespoon (15 ml) extra virgin
olive oil, divided

4 potato or brioche hamburger buns

16 pickle slices

The flavor from this avocado-ranch burger is incredible. You often think that more is better, but in this case it's the opposite. We don't need to pack this burger with lots of toppings. The flavors from the sweet and fluffy potato bread together with the chicken filet and dressing are more than enough.

Instructions

In a blender, add the sour cream, buttermilk, mayonnaise, dill, garlic, lemon juice and avocado. Blend until combined, then transfer the dressing to a bowl. Add the chives, salt and pepper, and stir until combined. Refrigerate the dressing until ready to serve.

Place the chicken on a cutting board. Use one hand to press it down while you cut horizontally all the way through the chicken to get four evenly thick filets (about ½ inch [1 cm]).

In a small bowl, mix the salt, garlic powder, pepper and paprika. Spread the spice mixture all over the chicken until the spices cover both sides of the filets.

Place the panko on a small plate. Place the beaten egg in a shallow bowl. Dip both chicken filets in the beaten egg, then the panko. Spray both sides of the chicken with cooking spray. Place the chicken in the air fryer, and cook on 355°F (180°C) for 14 to 15 minutes (or in an oven preheated to 355°F [180°C]).

When the chicken has about 4 minutes left, divide half of the olive oil among two large pans, and heat over medium heat. Place the hamburger buns cut side down in the pans, and cook until golden brown, about 2 minutes.

Place the bottom buns on four separate plates. Add 4 pickles to each bun, followed by a crispy chicken filet. Add 1 tablespoon (15 ml) of the Avocado-Ranch Dressing on the top bun for each burger, and place the bun on top of the chicken. Add a quarter of the leftover dressing to the side of each plate, preferably in a small shallow bowl to dip the burger in while eating.

FOR MEAT LOVERS

I've always been a meat lover, so it felt obvious to me to create a chapter dedicated to all the other meat lovers out there. Here you'll find a mix of my favorite recipes where meat is the star. Most of these dishes work perfectly when you want to turn your leftover meat into a whole new meal. You can experiment with what you have on hand, which makes these dishes great when you're cleaning out your refrigerator.

SIMPLE CHICKEN CURRY WRAP

Prep: 10 min
Cook: 15 min
Total: 25 min
Servings: 2

Ingredients

½ tablespoon (8 ml) extra virgin olive oil

8 ounces (226 g) boneless, skinless chicken breast, diced

½ Granny Smith apple, peeled and finely diced

2 tablespoons (6 g) chopped green onion

2 tablespoons (30 ml) mayonnaise

1 cup (240 ml) sour cream

1 tablespoon (6 g) yellow curry powder

1 tablespoon (15 g) sugar

1 teaspoon ground black pepper

2 large flour tortillas

2 cups (60 g) shredded lettuce, divided

Nothing beats a juicy chicken wrap for lunch. The special ingredient is green apple. It might sound odd, but the apple adds that little extra crunch, and its tartness balances all the flavors just perfectly. This recipe is a great way to turn leftover chicken into a whole new meal.

When I first made this recipe at home, it took me back to my teenage years when I always used to buy a baguette with this chicken filling after school. The sandwich place closed down, and that's when I decided to re-create this dish. I turned it into a wrap, and let me tell you, it's even better and the perfect lunch on the go!

Instructions

In a medium-sized pan over medium-high heat, place the olive oil. Add the chicken, and cook for about 5 minutes or until the chicken is cooked through. Transfer the chicken to a plate to cool.

In a large bowl, combine the apple, green onion, mayonnaise, sour cream, curry powder, sugar and pepper. Stir in the cooled chicken until it is coated in the dressing.

Heat the tortillas in the microwave for 10 to 15 seconds until softened. Place the tortillas next to each other on a clean, flat surface.

Add 1 cup (47 g) of the shredded lettuce in the center of each tortilla. Then add half of the chicken mixture on top of the lettuce in a line down the center of each tortilla.

Fold the sides over the filling, like wrapping a burrito. Roll the tortilla up over the filling, and tuck it in as you roll.

Notes: Put aluminum foil around the wrap if you're bringing it to go.

This filling is also great stuffing for a baked potato.

BEEF AND FETA CHEESE PIEROGIS

Prep: 15 min
Cook: 15 min
Total: 30 min
Servings: 4 pierogis

Ingredients

1 tablespoon (14 g) salted butter

½ small yellow onion, finely chopped

10½ ounces (300 g) ground beef

3½ ounces (93 g) cream cheese

½ teaspoon salt

1½ teaspoons (4 g) white pepper

2 teaspoons (2 g) dried oregano

1 (8-ounce [226-g]) can crescent roll dough, 8 count (or 1 crescent dough sheet)

8 tablespoons (76 g) feta cheese crumbles, divided

Chili flakes, to taste

1 egg, beaten

½ cup (120 ml) Garlic and Parmesan Sauce (page 134)

These pierogis are the perfect finger food. They're great as an appetizer, as a snack in front of the TV or as part of a buffet. This recipe is really simple to make and, by using store-bought crescent roll dough, they're done in no time. You can easily make the pierogis lacto-vegetarian by substituting ground beef for lightly fried spinach leaves. Serve with a side of my Garlic and Parmesan Sauce (page 134) for maximum flavor.

Instructions

Preheat the oven according to the dough package instructions. Line a baking sheet with parchment paper

Heat a medium-sized pan over medium heat. Add the butter and onion, and cook, stirring, for about 2 minutes. Increase the heat to medium-high, and add the ground beef. Cook, breaking up the meat, until brown, about 6 minutes.

Add the cream cheese to the pan, and mix for a minute or until melted and combined. Then add the salt, white pepper and oregano, and mix. Remove the pan from the heat.

If using crescent rolls, open them up, separate them into four equally large rectangles and pinch the diagonal cut in the middle of the rectangles to seal. If using a crescent dough sheet, open it up, and cut it into four equally large rectangles.

On one half of one rectangle, put a quarter of the ground beef mixture, and add 2 tablespoons (30 g) of the feta cheese crumbles on top. Sprinkle some chili flakes on top of the feta cheese. Fold the bare half of the crescent dough over the filling, making a small rectangle, and use a fork to press down the edges to close. Repeat with the rest of the dough.

Place the pierogis on the prepared baking sheet. Brush the beaten egg on top of the pierogis, and bake until golden brown, about 15 minutes or according to the crescent roll package instructions.

Cut the pierogis and serve with a side of Garlic and Parmesan Sauce.

JUICY CHICKEN BREAST WITH BAKED SWEET POTATO AND FETA CHEESE SAUCE

Prep: 5 min
Cook: 25 min
Total: 30 min
Servings: 2

Feta Cheese Sauce
½ cup (120 ml) sour cream

1 small clove garlic, minced

½ cup (75 g) feta cheese crumbles

¼ teaspoon salt

¼ teaspoon ground black pepper

½ teaspoon honey

Chicken and Sweet Potatoes
½ teaspoon salt

1 teaspoon garlic powder

¾ teaspoon ground black pepper

½ teaspoon paprika

2 (6-ounce [170-g]) boneless, skinless chicken breasts

1 tablespoon (14 g) salted butter

1 tablespoon (15 ml) extra virgin olive oil

2 (9½ ounce [270-g]) sweet potatoes, cleaned and dried

This recipe is the perfect combination of flavors. The sweetness from the sweet potato meets salty feta cheese and juicy, flavorful chicken breast. The secret to getting the chicken so juicy is to brown it quickly on high heat in lots of butter, and then finish it in the air fryer or oven.

Instructions

Make the Feta Cheese Sauce. In a small bowl, combine the sour cream, garlic, feta cheese, salt, pepper and honey. Refrigerate the cheese sauce until ready to serve.

In another small bowl, combine the salt, garlic powder, pepper and paprika. Rub the spice mixture over the chicken until well coated.

In a medium-sized pan over high heat, add the butter and olive oil. When the pan is very hot, add the chicken, and cook for about 1 minute on each side until a golden brown crust forms.

Remove the chicken from the pan, and place it in an air fryer on 355°F (180°C) (or in an oven preheated to 355°F [180°C]), and cook for 13 to 14 minutes.

Meanwhile, use a fork to poke small holes all over the sweet potatoes. Put the sweet potatoes on a paper towel and microwave uncovered for about 12 minutes, flipping halfway through. Remove the potatoes from the microwave (be careful since they're very hot), and cut a cross in the top of the potatoes. Gently pull apart the potatoes to open.

Once the chicken is done, cut it in slices, and plate it next to the sweet potatoes. Pour half of the cheese sauce inside each sweet potato and serve.

ONE-POT POTATO AND GROUND BEEF STEW

Prep: 10 min
Cook: 20 min
Total: 30 min
Servings: 4

Ingredients

1 tablespoon (14 g) salted butter

½ yellow onion, diced

1½ cups (185 g) diced zucchini

4 cloves garlic, minced

18 ounces (505 g) ground beef

1 tablespoon (15 ml) tomato paste

1 (14-ounce [410-g]) can crushed tomatoes

1 teaspoon sugar

1 teaspoon ground black pepper

¾ tablespoon (0.5 g) dried oregano

½ teaspoon chili flakes

1½–2 cups (360–480 ml) water

1 tablespoon (15 ml) soy sauce

2 vegetable bouillon cubes

14 ounces (400 g) potatoes, peeled and diced (about 4 large potatoes)

Sour cream, for serving

Fresh bread, for serving

A one-pot meal ready in 30 minutes is just what you need on a stressful weeknight. This recipe makes enough for the whole family, with maximum flavor and minimum cleanup.

Instructions

In a large pan with high sides, add the butter, and heat over medium heat. Once the butter starts to sizzle, add the onion and zucchini, and cook, stirring, for about 2 minutes. Add the garlic, and cook for 30 seconds more.

Transfer the onion mixture to a small bowl. In the same pan over medium-high heat, add the ground beef. Cook, breaking up the meat, until brown, about 6 minutes.

Make a hole in the center of the beef, and add the tomato paste. Cook for a few minutes until the tomato paste turns a darker color and smells sweet. Return the onion mixture to the pan with the beef, and stir to combine.

Add the crushed tomatoes, sugar, pepper, oregano and chili flakes, and mix until combined.

Pour the water into the can from the crushed tomatoes and add to the pan. Once the liquid starts to simmer, add the soy sauce and bouillon cubes. Stir to make sure the bouillon cubes dissolve.

Add the potatoes, making sure they're covered with the liquid. Cover the pan with a lid, and cook, stirring occasionally, until the potatoes are soft, 10 to 12 minutes.

Serve the stew with a spoonful of sour cream on top and some fresh bread on the side.

Note: Instead of serving with sour cream, you can add 8 ounces (232 g) of cream cheese to the stew at the end, mixing it in until melted. This will make the dish creamier.

TRIPLE MEAT SANDWICH

Prep: 5 min
Cook: 10 min
Total: 15 min
Servings: 2

Ingredients

4 slices bacon

4 slices whole wheat toast

2 tablespoons (30 ml) mayonnaise

4 lettuce leaves

4 thin tomato slices

Flaky sea salt, to taste

Ground black pepper, to taste

2 slices Colby Jack cheese

4 slices smoked deli ham, plus more to taste

1 teaspoon Dijon mustard

4 slices deli turkey breast, plus more to taste

1 avocado, mashed

I've never been much of a sandwich person, because I've never considered a sandwich a real meal. But I changed my mind after making this sandwich as a little snack and realizing it could easily have replaced my lunch. The next day I was already craving another one, and I made one for both me and my fiancé to bring to work. I wasn't surprised when he called me to let me know it was the best sandwich he'd ever had. And you know what's even better? There's absolutely no effort in making these.

Instructions

In a large pan, add the bacon, and heat it over high heat. When the bacon starts to sizzle, reduce the heat to medium-high, and cook until the bacon is crispy, 3 to 4 minutes. Remove the bacon from the pan, and place it on a paper towel or a rack to drain.

Lay the toast slices on a clean, flat surface.

Spread the mayonnaise on 2 pieces of toast; these will be the bottoms of the sandwiches.

On top of the mayonnaise, add 1 lettuce leaf, followed by half of the tomato, salt and black pepper to taste, 1 slice of cheese, half of the ham, half of the Dijon mustard, another lettuce leaf, half of the turkey and 2 slices of bacon. Repeat with the second sandwich.

Spread the mashed avocado on the 2 remaining pieces of toast, and put them on top of the bacon with the avocado facing the bacon. Use your hand to press down the sandwiches. Cut them in half diagonally and serve.

SIMPLE BEEF AND NOODLE STIR-FRY

Sauce

2 tablespoons (30 ml) soy sauce

2 teaspoons (10 ml) sesame oil

2 large cloves garlic

1 tablespoon (15 ml) honey

1 tablespoon (15 ml) lime juice

½ cup (120 ml) oyster sauce

Stir-Fry

1 tablespoon (15 ml) canola oil, divided

½ red onion, sliced

11 ounces (312 g) ground beef

½ teaspoon ground black pepper

3 ounces (85 g) bite-sized broccoli florets

6 ounces (170 g) shredded carrots

½ red bell pepper, chopped

7 ounces (200 g) lo mein noodles

Chili flakes, for serving

The sauce in this stir-fry is sweet, salty and tart, and it actually tastes even better the next day, so it's perfect to bring to work. This is also a great dish when cleaning out the fridge, since you can change up the vegetables and meat.

Instructions

Make the sauce. In a small bowl, combine the soy sauce, sesame oil, garlic, honey, lime juice and oyster sauce. Set aside.

In a large pan with high sides, add ½ tablespoon (7.5 ml) of the canola oil, and heat over medium heat. Add the onion, and cook, stirring occasionally, until it starts to soften, about 3 minutes. Transfer the onion to a large bowl.

Return the pan to the stove over medium-high heat. Add the ground beef and pepper. Cook, breaking up the meat, until brown, about 6 minutes. Transfer the beef to the bowl with the onion.

Return the pan to the stove over medium-low heat. Place in the remaining ½ tablespoon (7.5 ml) of canola oil and the broccoli. Cook, stirring once every minute, for 5 minutes. Add the carrots and red pepper. Cook for another 5 to 7 minutes or until the vegetables reach your preferred texture (I don't like mine too soft).

Meanwhile, bring a pot of water to a boil, and cook the lo mein noodles according to package instructions. Drain the noodles and set aside.

Once the vegetables are done, return the ground beef and onion back to the pan, followed by the stir-fry sauce. Mix everything, then add the noodles and toss. Serve with chili flakes to taste.

GARLIC AND PARMESAN CHICKEN SANDWICH

Prep: 10 min
Cook: 20 min
Total: 30 min
Servings: 4

Ingredients

8 slices bacon

2 (8-ounce [226-g]) boneless, skinless chicken breasts

¼ teaspoon salt

½ teaspoon garlic powder

½ teaspoon paprika

8 slices sourdough bread

½ cup (120 ml) Garlic and Parmesan Sauce (page 134)

4 lettuce leaves

8 fine tomato slices

½ small red onion, finely sliced

About a year ago, I worked as a teacher's assistant at a high school restaurant program, and every Friday they made sandwiches for the school café. One of these sandwiches looked so good, I just had to try and re-create it. This Garlic and Parmesan Chicken Sandwich has become my new obsession. The key is using a fresh, juicy chicken breast and cutting your own slices of bread from a loaf of sourdough.

Instructions

In a large pan, add the bacon, and heat it over high heat. When the bacon starts to sizzle, reduce the heat to medium-high, and cook until the bacon is crispy, 3 to 4 minutes. Remove the bacon from the pan, and place it on a paper towel or a rack to drain. Leave the bacon fat in the pan.

Place the chicken on a cutting board. Use one hand to press it down while you cut horizontally all the way through the chicken to get 4 evenly thick filets (about ½ inch [1 cm]).

In a small bowl, combine the salt, garlic powder and paprika. Cover both sides of the chicken filets with the spice mix.

Heat the pan with the bacon fat over medium heat. Add the chicken, and cook, flipping halfway, until cooked through, about 6 minutes.

Toast the bread, and place 2 slices of bread on one plate for each sandwich. Spread 1 tablespoon (15 ml) of the Garlic and Parmesan Sauce on 1 piece of bread for each plate.

On top of the sauce, add 1 lettuce leaf, 2 tomato slices, a quarter of the red onion, 2 slices of bacon and 1 chicken filet. Drizzle another tablespoon (15 ml) of the sauce over the chicken. Put the second slice of bread on top, repeat with the remaining sandwich ingredients and serve.

CREAMY BEEF TENDERLOIN PASTA

Prep: 10 min
Cook: 20 min
Total: 30 min
Servings: 2

Ingredients
6 ounces (170 g) penne

2½ tablespoons (35 g) salted butter, divided

1 shallot, finely chopped

3½ ounces (100 g) thinly sliced champignon mushrooms

1 large clove garlic, minced

7 ounces (200 g) beef tenderloin, sliced (about 1 x 1½-inch [2.5 x 4-cm] slices)

½ cup (120 ml) red wine (cooking wine is fine)

¾ cup (180 ml) heavy cream

1 tablespoon (15 ml) soy sauce

¼ teaspoon cayenne pepper, plus more to taste

Salt, to taste

Grated Parmesan cheese, for garnish

Fresh parsley leaves, for garnish

This creamy pasta with beef tenderloin and mushrooms is perfect for a weekend dinner. It might sound fancy, but it's so simple to make. It's a real favorite in my house, and perfect to serve any guests that come over.

Instructions

Bring a pot of salted water to boil, and cook the pasta according to box instructions. Before draining, reserve 2 tablespoons (30 ml) of the pasta water.

In a large pan with high sides over medium heat, add 2 tablespoons (14 g) of the butter. Add the shallot and mushrooms, and cook, stirring occasionally, until the mushrooms have softened, about 3 minutes. Add the garlic, and cook, stirring, for another minute. Transfer the vegetables to a bowl and set aside.

Return the pan to the stove over high heat, and add another ½ tablespoon (7 g) of butter. Add the beef, and brown for about 1 minute. Remove the meat from the pan.

Reduce the heat to medium-low, and pour the red wine into the pan. Let it simmer for 4 to 5 minutes, and scrape the brown bits from the bottom of the pan.

Return the vegetables to the pan. Add the heavy cream, soy sauce and cayenne pepper, and mix everything together. Let it simmer for 2 to 3 minutes, stirring occasionally and scraping the bottom of the pan, until the sauce thickens. Add the pasta water and season with salt to taste.

Add the beef back to the pan, and stir to coat it with the sauce. Cook until the sauce is heated through, then add the drained pasta, and toss.

Serve with grated Parmesan cheese and some fresh parsley.

EAT YOUR GREENS

I love all greens and vegetables, but for some reason I've always been bad at eating enough, which inspired me to create these recipes. In some of these dishes, the vegetables are hidden and blended, which makes them perfect to serve to anyone who's picky with their greens. This is a really fun and simple way to get your vitamins and fiber. But that doesn't mean my recipes are cheap on the flavors. Curry, lime, coconut, honey, chili and garlic are just a few, and the dishes in this chapter are inspired by flavors from different countries.

HIDDEN VEGGIE PASTA

Prep: 5 min
Cook: 25 min
Total: 30 min
Servings: 5 to 6

Ingredients

1 red onion

3 carrots

9 ounces (255 g) cherry tomatoes

1 red chili pepper, chopped (optional)

3 large cloves garlic, peeled

2 tablespoons (30 ml) extra virgin olive oil

½ teaspoon ground black pepper

1 teaspoon dried oregano

17 ounces (480 g) uncooked short-shaped pasta

1 vegetable bouillon cube

½ tablespoon (8 g) sugar

7 ounces (200 g) cream cheese

1 cup (10 g) fresh basil leaves

½ teaspoon salt, plus more to taste

Grated Parmesan cheese, for garnish

Ever wondered how to get your kids to eat more vegetables? Or maybe you need those extra vitamins? Do you love a creamy pasta as much as I do? Then this recipe is for you! The best thing about this dish is, besides boiling pasta, the oven and blender will be doing the cooking for you.

Instructions

Preheat the oven to 440°F (225°C). Peel the onion and cut it into 4 pieces. Cut the carrots into ½-inch (1-cm)–thick circles (leave the peel on; we want those vitamins).

In an oven-safe baking dish, spread out all the vegetables. Add the olive oil, pepper and oregano, and mix to coat the vegetables. Bake for 20 minutes.

Meanwhile, bring a pot of salted water to boil, and cook the pasta according to the box instructions. Drain.

Remove the baking dish from the oven, and transfer the vegetables to a heat-resistant blender.

Add the bouillon cube, sugar, cream cheese, basil and salt, and blend until smooth, about 1 minute.

Pour the vegetable sauce all over the drained pasta, and toss. Serve with a generous amount of grated Parmesan cheese.

Note: Try experimenting with the vegetables. Add or substitute for some of your favorites!

MIXED SUMMER SALAD

Prep: 20 min
Cook: 10 min
Total: 30 min
Servings: 5 to 6

Dressing

4 tablespoons (60 ml) extra virgin olive oil

2 tablespoons (30 ml) balsamic vinegar

½ teaspoon ground black pepper

½ teaspoon dried oregano (see Note)

¼ teaspoon salt

Salad

8 slices bacon, chopped

1¾ ounces (50 g) pine nuts

1 tablespoon (15 ml) extra virgin olive oil

13 ounces (370 g) fresh asparagus, cut into 1½-inch (4-cm) pieces

¼ teaspoon flaky sea salt

¼ teaspoon garlic powder

Rotisserie chicken, skin and bones removed (about 12 ounces [340 g] chicken meat)

3 cups (450 g) diced watermelon

1¼ cups (240 g) diced feta cheese

3 cups (500 g) diced peaches

4 cups (200 g) chopped crisp lettuce

9 ounces (255 g) halved grape tomatoes

As the name suggests, this is a perfect summer salad. When it's hot outside, a cold salad is all I want to eat, and I'm obsessed with this one. The flavorful fried asparagus, chicken and bacon, together with the fresh, sweet watermelon and peaches, make a delicious combination. You can replace the chicken and bacon for fried halloumi to make this salad lacto-vegetarian. You can also omit the meat, making this great to serve as a side salad to your main dish.

Instructions

Make the dressing. In a small glass jar, combine the olive oil, balsamic vinegar, pepper, oregano and salt, and set aside.

Make the salad. In a large pan, place the bacon, and heat it over high heat. When the bacon starts to sizzle, reduce the heat to medium-high, and cook until the bacon is crispy, 3 to 4 minutes. Remove the bacon from the pan, and place it on a paper towel to drain.

Heat a small pan over low heat, and place in the pine nuts. Toast, stirring often, until the pine nuts are light brown, about 5 minutes. Remove from the heat and set aside.

Heat the olive oil in a large pan over medium heat, and add the asparagus, salt and garlic powder. Cook, stirring often, for about 5 minutes. Remove from the heat and set aside.

In a large bowl, combine the bacon, asparagus, chicken, watermelon, feta, peaches, lettuce and tomatoes. Add the dressing and toss, or serve the dressing on the side.

Top the salad with the pine nuts and serve.

Note: Before adding the oregano, rub it in between your fingers to release the oils.

AVOCADO TOAST WITH PESTO EGGS

Prep: 10 min
Cook: 10 min
Total: 20 min
Servings: 2

Ingredients

2 avocados, mashed

½ cup (75 g) finely chopped tomato

1 tablespoon (10 g) finely chopped red onion

¼ teaspoon lemon pepper (see Note)

Pinch of salt

2 tablespoons (30 ml) pesto (store-bought or homemade [page 30]), divided

2 eggs

2 slices whole grain bread

Salted butter

Chili flakes, to taste

Let's talk about classic avocado toast. It doesn't matter if it's for breakfast, lunch or a snack. A crispy buttered bread with smooth avocado spread is always a good idea. Even if it's already one of the most delicious toasts, I take it to the next level with this recipe inspired by the viral TikTok trend. The perfectly cooked pesto egg provides extra protein and tons of flavor.

Instructions

In a medium bowl, combine the avocados, tomato, red onion, lemon pepper and salt, and set aside.

Heat a large nonstick pan over medium heat. Add 1 tablespoon (15 ml) of the pesto on each side of the pan. Gently spread the pesto in circular motions with the back of a spoon until you have two circles the size of a fried egg (about 4 inches [10 cm] across).

Crack an egg on top of each pesto circle, and cook for 1 minute. Cover the pan with a lid, and cook for 2 minutes more, or until the white is set and the yolk is still runny. Remove the eggs from the pan.

Meanwhile, toast the bread. Place each piece of toast on two separate plates, and butter the side facing up.

Add half of the avocado mixture to each slice of toast, and place the pesto eggs on top. Finish off with some chili flakes to taste.

Notes: Mix it up! Instead of the pesto eggs, top the mashed avocado mix with salty feta cheese crumbles and sweet pomegranate seeds.

If you don't have lemon pepper, you can substitute ¼ teaspoon of ground black pepper and ¼ teaspoon of lemon juice.

CREAMY POTATO AND BROCCOLI-CHEDDAR SOUP

Ingredients

2 tablespoons (28 g) salted butter

1 yellow onion, diced

4 large potatoes, diced

2 cloves garlic, chopped

2½ cups (600 ml) water

2 cups (480 ml) heavy cream

18 ounces (510 g) frozen broccoli florets

2 vegetable bouillon cubes

2½ cups (280 g) freshly shredded Cheddar cheese, divided

Salt, to taste

White pepper, to taste

Rich and cheesy Cheddar meets broccoli and makes the perfect combination in this recipe. This soup is my favorite of all time. It's as good freshly made for a weeknight dinner as it is the next day for leftovers. This is the dish I make whenever I want something simple that's not too heavy yet still filling. Top it off with some more cheese and enjoy with a side of buttered, freshly baked bread.

Instructions

Heat a large pot over medium heat. Add the butter, onion and potatoes, and cook, stirring, for about 3 minutes. Add the garlic, and cook for another minute.

Increase the heat to high. Add the water and heavy cream to the pot, and bring to a boil.

Add the broccoli and bouillon cubes, reduce the heat back to medium and partially cover the pot with a lid. Simmer until the broccoli and potatoes are soft, about 5 minutes, stirring occasionally.

Remove the pot from the heat, and use a handheld blender to blend the soup until smooth, about 1 minute. (You can also use a stationary blender; just make sure it's heat resistant.)

Return the pot to the stove over medium heat, and add 2 cups (226 g) of the Cheddar cheese. Stir until the cheese is melted, about 1 minute. Season with salt and white pepper to taste.

Divide the soup into bowls, and top it off with the remaining Cheddar cheese for garnish.

Note: If you like a little texture, toast some pine nuts in a pan over low heat until golden brown, about 5 minutes, and use for garnish together with the Cheddar cheese, or add some extra broccoli florets to the soup after mixing.

LETTUCE-WRAPPED FISH TACOS WITH MANGO AND AVOCADO SALSA

Prep: 10 min
Cook: 20 min
Total: 30 min
Servings: 4

Mango and Avocado Salsa

2 cups (200 g) finely diced mango

2 avocados, finely diced

4 tablespoons (40 g) finely chopped red onion

2 teaspoons (6 g) finely chopped red chili pepper

4 tablespoons (60 ml) lime juice

1 tablespoon (15 ml) extra virgin olive oil

2 tablespoons (2 g) fresh chopped cilantro leaves

¼ teaspoon salt

Fish Tacos

15 ounces (425 g) cod filets, sliced (about 3 x 1-inch [7 x 2½-cm] slices)

Salt

Ground black pepper

¼ cup (30 g) wheat flour

½ cup (28 g) panko

1 egg, beaten

3 tablespoons (45 ml) canola oil

8 lettuce leaves

½ cup (75 g) feta cheese crumbles, divided

4 tablespoons (60 ml) Sriracha Mayonnaise (page 82)

If I say *taco*, you might think of the ordinary beef or chicken taco. But there're so many different ways to make tacos. The word *taco* actually means a tortilla filled with mixed ingredients, so I like to play around with it. In this recipe, I swap the tortilla for lettuce to create a greener dish. The star of this dish is from the sea and tastes so good together with the tart, sweet and spicy mango and avocado salsa. If you want to make this recipe even simpler, you can use store-bought fish sticks. Remember that it's OK to not always have time or energy, and cooking should be simple and fun!

Instructions

In a medium-sized bowl, combine the mango, avocados, red onion, red chili pepper, lime juice, olive oil, cilantro and salt. Refrigerate until ready to serve.

Pat the fish dry with a paper towel, and cover both sides of the fish with a generous amount of salt and pepper.

Add the flour and panko to two separate plates, and place the bowl with beaten egg in between them. Dredge each piece of fish in flour, then egg and then panko.

In a large pan over medium heat, place the canola oil. Add the fish, and cook until golden brown, about 2 minutes per side. Remove the fish, and assemble the tacos immediately by placing the lettuce leaves on four separate plates, 2 for each plate, and fill each with ⅛ of the fish and salsa. Add 1 tablespoon (10 g) of the feta cheese crumbles for each taco, drizzle the Sriracha Mayonnaise on top and serve.

Note: You can substitute bread crumbs for the panko if needed.

SIMPLE PASTA SALAD

Prep: 15 min
Cook: 15 min
Total: 30 min
Servings: 4

Salad

7 ounces (200 g) farfalle

¹/₃ cup (50 g) pine nuts

1¼ cups (150 g) diced feta cheese (you can substitute this for halved mozzarella balls)

7 ounces (200 g) halved grape tomatoes

1½ cups (180 g) diced cucumber

1½ cups (223 g) diced red bell pepper

2 avocados, diced

½ red onion, thinly sliced

2 cups (60 g) baby spinach

4 cups (240 g) fully cooked diced ham

Dressing

²/₃ cup (160 ml) sour cream

¼ cup (60 ml) Thai sweet chili sauce

½ teaspoon garlic powder

¹/₈ teaspoon salt

¼ teaspoon ground black pepper

This is a super simple pasta salad that you can make in no time. It's full of fresh ingredients and packed with flavor. I love the different textures from the crispy vegetables, creamy feta cheese and crunchy pine nuts. You can use substitute ingredients, switch it up and at times just use what you have at home. You can easily make this several times a week without getting tired of it, and it's the perfect meal on the go since it's served cold.

Instructions

Bring a pot of salted water to boil, and cook the pasta according to box instructions. Drain the pasta, rinse under cold water and set it aside to cool.

Meanwhile, in a medium bowl, combine the sour cream, Thai sweet chili sauce, garlic powder, salt and pepper, and set aside.

Heat a small pan over low heat, and add the pine nuts. Toast the pine nuts until they are light brown, about 5 minutes, stirring often so they don't burn. Remove the pan from the heat.

In a large bowl, combine the drained pasta, feta, tomatoes, cucumber, bell pepper, avocados, red onion, spinach and ham. Toss until everything is mixed. Add the dressing and toss to coat, or serve it on the side.

Top the salad with the pine nuts and serve.

HONEY–LIME SALMON WITH FRIED BROCCOLI

Prep: 5 min
Cook: 25 min
Total: 30 min
Servings: 2

Honey–Lime Marinade

2 tablespoons (30 ml) canola oil

2 teaspoons (10 ml) lime juice

1 large clove garlic, minced

½ teaspoon salt

1 teaspoon (5 ml) soy sauce

1 teaspoon (5 ml) Worcestershire sauce

¼ teaspoon cayenne pepper

1½ tablespoons (23 ml) honey

Salmon and Broccoli

9 ounces (255 g) fresh broccoli florets, cut in bite-sized pieces

2 tablespoons (30 ml) extra virgin olive oil

Salt, to taste

9 ounces (255 g) salmon (2 filets)

1 tablespoon (14 g) salted butter

1 teaspoon toasted sesame seeds, for serving

The flavors from this honey and lime marinade are out of this world. When I first made it, I honestly marinated everything I could find in my refrigerator because it was so good. There's nothing like brushing the marinade on the salmon and placing it in a hot pan to get that golden, flavorful crust. The salmon is also great on top of glass noodles or rice.

Instructions

In a small bowl, combine the canola oil, lime juice, garlic, salt, soy sauce, Worcestershire sauce, cayenne and honey, and set aside.

In a large frying pan over high heat, add the broccoli florets, olive oil and a pinch of salt to taste. Stir to coat the broccoli. Once the broccoli starts to sizzle, reduce the heat to medium-low, and cook, stirring often, for about 12 minutes or until the broccoli has softened but still has a bit of texture.

While the broccoli is cooking, pat the salmon filets dry with a paper towel.

In a medium-sized pan over medium-high heat, add the butter. Brush the Honey–Lime Marinade on the salmon until it is covered, reserving 2 teaspoons (10 ml), and add the filets to the pan. Cook the salmon on both sides for about 1 minute each to get a golden-brown crust, but make sure the marinade doesn't burn.

Remove the salmon from the pan, and brush more marinade onto both sides. Place the salmon in the air fryer on 355°F (180°C), and cook for about 5 minutes (or in an oven preheated to 355°F [180°C]). Take the salmon out halfway through the cooking time, and brush more marinade on each filet.

Before removing the broccoli florets, drizzle 1 teaspoon of the marinade over them, and toss to coat.

Place each salmon filet on a separate plate, and add half of the broccoli florets to each plate. Brush the remaining marinade on the salmon, and sprinkle with the sesame seeds.

CARROT AND RED LENTIL SOUP

Ingredients

1 tablespoon (15 ml) extra virgin olive oil

1 yellow onion, diced

2 cloves garlic, chopped

1-inch (2.5-cm) piece ginger, grated

½ teaspoon chili flakes, plus more to taste

15 ounces (410 g) carrots (sliced into ½-inch [1-cm]–thick disks)

2¼ cups (540 ml) coconut milk

2 tablespoons (30 ml) lemon juice

½ tablespoon (8 ml) lime juice

1 to 2 teaspoons yellow curry powder

1 cup (192 g) red lentils

7 ounces (200 g) peeled and diced sweet potato

2 ounces (56 g) unsweetened coconut chips

1½ teaspoons (9 g) salt

1 teaspoon ground black pepper

Fresh cilantro leaves, for garnish

I'm definitely a soup lover. You can basically make soup out of anything. My Carrot and Red Lentil Soup is so simple because it's made all in one pot. This creamy soup has flavors from coconut, lime and yellow curry. Leftovers are even more flavorful the next day. This soup is low in fat and packed with vitamins, iron, fiber and protein from the vegetables and lentils.

Instructions

In a large pot, add the olive oil, and heat over medium heat. Once the oil is hot, add the onion, and cook for about 2 minutes. Add the garlic, ginger and chili flakes, and cook, stirring, for another minute.

Add the carrots, coconut milk, 2¼ cups (540 ml) water, lemon and lime juices and curry powder to the pot. Add the red lentils. Increase the heat to high, partially cover the pot with a lid and bring the mixture to a simmer. Reduce the heat to medium, and cook for 5 minutes. Carefully add the sweet potatoes, and cook until the carrots, lentils and sweet potatoes are soft, about 5 minutes more. Stir occasionally to prevent the lentils from sticking to the bottom.

Meanwhile, heat a small pan over medium-low heat. Add the coconut chips, and toast them until they are a light golden brown color, 3 to 4 minutes. Stir frequently to prevent the chips from burning.

Remove the pot from the heat, and use a handheld blender to blend the soup until smooth, about 1 minute. Once blended, stir in the salt and black pepper.

Serve the soup topped with the toasted coconut chips and, if preferred, some more chili flakes to taste. Garnish with cilantro.

SWEET POTATO SOUP

Prep: 10 min
Cook: 15 min
Total: 25 min
Servings: 5 to 6

Ingredients

1 tablespoon (15 ml) extra virgin olive oil

1 yellow onion, diced

2 cloves garlic, chopped

½ teaspoon chili flakes, plus more to taste

28 ounces (785 g) peeled and diced sweet potatoes

2 cups (480 ml) coconut milk

2 tablespoons (30 ml) lime juice

2 ounces (56 g) pumpkin seeds

1¾ teaspoons (10 g) salt

½ teaspoon ground black pepper

This dish has lots of delicious flavors from coconut milk, lime and chili. I've been a sweet potato lover for years, but still it never occurred to me until recently that I should turn it into a soup. Let me tell you, I've been missing out. This is now one of my favorite lunches to make.

Instructions

In a large pot, add the olive oil, and heat over medium heat. Once the oil is hot, add the onion, and cook for about 2 minutes. Add the garlic and chili flakes, and cook, stirring, for another minute.

Add the sweet potatoes, coconut milk, 2 cups (480 ml) water and lime juice. Increase the heat to high, partially cover the pot with a lid and bring to a simmer. Reduce the heat to medium, and cook until the sweet potatoes are soft, about 5 minutes.

Meanwhile, heat a small pan over medium-low heat. Add the pumpkin seeds and toast them for 3 to 4 minutes, stirring frequently to prevent them from burning.

Once the sweet potatoes are soft, remove the pot from the heat, and use a handheld blender to blend the soup until smooth, about 1 minute. Stir in the salt and black pepper.

Serve the soup topped with the toasted pumpkin seeds.

SNACKS AND SIDES

In this chapter you'll find some of my favorite snacks and sides. They're a great way to satisfy your late-night cravings, or to have as a side to your main dish. My favorite thing to do is serve a bunch of small dishes like these as a main course, inspired by the Spanish tapas, where everyone can sit together around the table and share food. You can serve a few of these dishes before dinner by setting up a small table where people can go and grab a little now and then. It's a lot more casual than a sit-down appetizer and will give everyone a chance to mingle at the same time.

THE BEST GARLIC BREAD

Garlic Butter
3 ounces (85 g) salted butter

3 ounces (85 g) cream cheese

½ teaspoon lemon juice

¼ teaspoon chili powder

½ teaspoon paprika

¼ teaspoon dried dill

¼ teaspoon flaky sea salt

5 small cloves garlic, minced

Garlic Bread
1 (20-inch [50-cm]) French baguette

1 cup (112 g) shredded mozzarella

I don't know anyone who can resist the smell of this garlic bread. I've grown up with it, since my mom made it as an appetizer every Friday dinner. Most of the time my brother and I ate so much that by dinner we were already full. Now I've decided to re-create the recipe for my family, putting my own little twist on it. I just have to warn you before you make it: This bread is addictive, and you won't be able to stop eating it.

Instructions
Preheat the oven to 430°F (220°C). Line a baking sheet with parchment paper.

Make the garlic butter. In a medium-sized bowl, combine the butter, cream cheese, lemon juice, chili powder, paprika, dill, salt and garlic, and mix well to incorporate.

Cut off the ends of the baguette, and slice the rest of the baguette into 4 pieces, each about 4 inches (10 cm) long. Slice each piece horizontally all the way through.

Spread the garlic butter all over the insides of the baguette slices, and add 2 tablespoons (14 g) of the shredded mozzarella to each one.

Brush some cold water on the bottoms of each slice of bread. This will make them crispy.

Place the baguette slices on the prepared baking sheet, and bake for 6 to 8 minutes or until the bread is a light golden brown color. Serve immediately.

Note: If you like Parmesan with your garlic bread, add ½ cup (28 g) of finely grated Parmesan cheese to the garlic butter.

AIR-FRIED POTATO WEDGES WITH CHIPOTLE MAYONNAISE

Prep: 0 min
Cook: 30 min
Total: 30 min
Servings: 2

Potato Wedges
18 ounces (510 g) russet potatoes

½ tablespoon (8 ml) extra virgin olive oil

¾ teaspoon salt (see Note)

½ teaspoon ground black pepper

½ teaspoon garlic powder

¾ teaspoon dried thyme

Chipotle Mayonnaise
¼ cup (60 ml) mayonnaise

1½ tablespoons (23 ml) ketchup

¼ teaspoon garlic powder

½ teaspoon chipotle powder

These potatoes require minimal effort and they're so good. The air fryer will do the work for you, and there's no need to peel the potatoes, since they will get even crispier with the peel on. These potato wedges are great by themselves but are also perfect as a side for a juicy steak dinner or a greasy burger.

Instructions

Wash the potatoes, and cut them in half lengthwise, then cut each half into three wedges (about ¾ inch [2 cm] thick).

In a large bowl, add the potato wedges, olive oil, salt, pepper, garlic powder and thyme. Toss until all wedges are covered.

Pour the wedges into the air fryer, and spread them out as much as possible. Depending on the size of your air fryer, you might have to do these in batches.

Air fry on 365°F (185°C) for 15 minutes. Stir the potatoes around the air fryer, increase the temperature to 400°F (200°C), and air fry for another 5 minutes.

Meanwhile, make the chipotle mayonnaise. In a small bowl combine the mayonnaise, ketchup, garlic powder and chipotle powder, and set aside.

Serve the potato wedges hot with a side of chipotle mayonnaise for dipping.

Notes: If you like your potato wedges saltier, wait and add the salt after the wedges are cooked.

Cheese them up! After the first 15 minutes of cook time, transfer the potatoes to a bowl, and toss them with finely grated Parmesan cheese, then return to the air fryer and follow the steps above.

ADDICTIVE GUACAMOLE

Prep: 10 min
Cook: 5 min
Total: 15 min
Servings: 2

Ingredients

2 avocados, mashed

1½ teaspoons (8 ml) lime juice

2 tablespoons (30 ml) sour cream

1 clove garlic, minced

¼ teaspoon cayenne pepper, plus more to taste

½ cup (75 g) finely chopped tomato (about ½ small tomato)

1 tablespoon (10 g) finely chopped red onion

½ tablespoon (1 g) finely chopped fresh cilantro leaves

Pinch of flaky sea salt

Nacho chips, for serving

When I went to Mexico for vacation a few years ago, I became obsessed with guacamole. Ever since then I've made it at home at least once a week. In Sweden, people have very mixed feelings about dairy in guacamole, since there isn't any in the original recipe. I used to make mine without sour cream, but the more I've tried this version the more I like it, and now I won't make my guacamole without it. It brings that extra creaminess and flavor to the guacamole that goes so well with all the other ingredients. If you're not a fan, don't worry—just leave it out. But promise me you'll try it first; you won't regret it.

Instructions

In a medium-sized bowl, combine the avocado, lime juice, sour cream, garlic, cayenne pepper, tomato, red onion, cilantro and salt. Mix everything together and serve with nacho chips.

Note: Did you know that you can make your own nacho chips in the air fryer? Just brush both sides of a large corn tortilla with a mix of 1 tablespoon (15 ml) of extra virgin olive oil and ¼ teaspoon each of salt, chili powder, garlic powder and paprika powder. Cut the tortilla in triangles, and air fry for 7 to 8 minutes on 350°F (175°C).

AVOCADO AND CREAM CHEESE-FILLED CUCUMBERS

Prep: 5 min
Cook: 15 min
Total: 20 min
Servings: 2

Ingredients
¼ teaspoon chili flakes

¼ teaspoon garlic powder

¼ teaspoon toasted white sesame seeds

¼ teaspoon black sesame seeds

1 cucumber, peeled

4 slices bacon, chopped

8 tablespoons (115 g) cream cheese

1 large avocado, mashed

Flaky sea salt

Filled "cucumber boats" are the perfect low-carb snack, appetizer or finger food for any event. When I was pregnant and had completely lost my appetite, these filled cucumbers were all I could eat, since they're so refreshing. Even though there are only a few ingredients, they have vitamins, minerals and healthy fats.

Instructions
In a small bowl, mix the chili flakes, garlic powder and white and black sesame seeds.

Cut the cucumber in half, and then divide the two halves horizontally.

Use a teaspoon to scrape out the inside of the cucumber, and pat it dry with a paper towel. You'll now have four "cucumber boats."

Place the bacon in a large pan, and heat over high heat. When the bacon starts to sizzle, reduce the heat to medium-high, and cook until the bacon is crispy, 3 to 4 minutes. Remove the bacon from the pan, and place it on a paper towel to drain.

Spread a quarter of the cream cheese on the inside of 1 cucumber, and add a quarter of the mashed avocado on top. Take a pinch of flaky sea salt, and rub it between your fingertips over the mashed avocado.

Add a quarter of the spice mixture on top of the avocado, followed by a quarter of the bacon crumbles.

Repeat with the remaining ingredients.

Note: If you want to make these a little fancier, cut the cucumber in smaller pieces after adding all the toppings, and substitute the bacon for slices of cold smoked salmon.

CORNFLAKE-CRUSTED CHICKEN TENDERS WITH GARLIC AND PARMESAN SAUCE

Prep: 5 min
Cook: 25 min
Total: 30 min
Servings: 2

Garlic and Parmesan Sauce (makes ½ cup [120 ml])

6 tablespoons (90 ml) sour cream

1½ tablespoons (23 ml) mayonnaise

¼ cup (25 g) finely grated Parmesan cheese

1 small clove garlic, minced

⅛ teaspoon salt

⅛ teaspoon ground black pepper

Chicken Tenders

1 teaspoon salt

1 tablespoon (8 g) garlic powder

2 teaspoons (4 g) ground black pepper

2 teaspoons (4 g) paprika

14 ounces (400 g) boneless, skinless chicken tenderloins

1¾ cups (130 g) Cornflakes

2 eggs, beaten

2 tablespoons (30 ml) canola oil

This chicken is juicy on the inside and crispy on the outside! The secret to this recipe is covering the chicken with Cornflakes. And how did I come up with this genius idea? Well, I didn't really. I was making chicken tenders one day, and I realized I forgot to buy the ingredients for the breading. I immediately started to think of other options that I might have at home, and I found Cornflakes. Lucky me, because this recipe is something extra! Together with my favorite dipping sauce, I just can't get enough.

Instructions

Make the sauce. In a small bowl, combine the sour cream, mayonnaise, Parmesan, garlic, salt and pepper, and set aside.

Make the spice rub for the chicken. In another small bowl, combine the salt, garlic powder, pepper and paprika. Spread the spice mixture over the chicken tenders until they're well covered.

Crush the Cornflakes and place in a shallow bowl. Place the bowl with beaten eggs next to the Cornflakes.

Dredge the chicken first in the egg, then in the Cornflakes.

Add the oil to a large pan, and heat over medium heat. Once the oil is hot, add the chicken, and cook for 1 minute on each side to get a nice crust. Then remove the chicken, place it in the air fryer on 355°F (180°C) and cook for 5 minutes (or in an oven preheated to 355°F [180°C]).

Serve the crispy chicken tenders immediately with the Garlic and Parmesan Sauce.

DIRTY JALAPEÑO AND CHEDDAR CHEESE FRIES

Prep: 10 min
Cook: 15 to 20 min
Total: 25 to 30 min
Servings: 4

Dirty Fries
23 ounces (650 g) frozen crinkle-cut French fries

8 slices bacon, chopped

4 tablespoons (55 g) salted butter (½ stick)

2 tablespoons (16 g) whole wheat flour

¾ cup (180 ml) low-fat milk

1 teaspoon paprika

2 cups (180 g) freshly shredded Cheddar cheese

6 tablespoons (60 g) finely chopped pickled jalapeños

½ teaspoon salt

¼ teaspoon cayenne pepper

½ teaspoon garlic powder

2 tablespoons (20 g) finely chopped red onion

Chipotle Mayonnaise
½ cup (120 ml) mayonnaise

3 tablespoons (45 ml) ketchup

½ teaspoon garlic powder

1 teaspoon chipotle powder

Take your fries to a whole new level with this dirty fries recipe. The homemade melted cheese sauce with real Cheddar is so much better than the one you'll get from a fast-food place. Crispy bacon crumbles, jalapeños and onions are just some of the many toppings you can choose from. When I serve these, everyone wants more, and I can't wait for you to try them.

Instructions
Cook the French fries according to package instructions.

Meanwhile, make the chipotle mayonnaise. In a small bowl, combine the mayonnaise, ketchup, garlic powder and chipotle powder, and set aside.

Place the bacon in a large pan, and heat it over high heat. When the bacon starts to sizzle, reduce the heat to medium-high and cook, stirring frequently, until the bacon is crispy, 3 to 4 minutes. Remove the bacon from the pan, and place it on a paper towel to drain.

In a medium-sized pot, place the butter, and heat over medium heat. Once the butter starts to sizzle, reduce the heat to medium-low. Whisk in the flour until well incorporated.

Add the milk and paprika, and cook, whisking, for about 30 seconds. Add the cheese, and stir until melted, about 1 minute. Add the jalapeños and remove the pot from the heat.

In a large bowl, combine the fries, salt, cayenne pepper and garlic powder, and toss to coat.

Plate the fries, and pour the cheese sauce all over them. Top with the red onion and bacon crumbles. Drizzle the chipotle mayonnaise over the fries, or serve on the side.

FRIED GARLIC TOMATOES AND RICOTTA CHEESE TOAST

Prep: 5 min
Cook: 15 min
Total: 20 min
Servings: 4

Ingredients
1½ tablespoons (23 ml) extra virgin olive oil

18 ounces (510 g) small cherry tomatoes, halved

2 cloves garlic, minced

4 slices sourdough bread

8 ounces (230 g) whole-milk ricotta cheese

2 handfuls arugula

Flaky sea salt, to taste

Ground black pepper, to taste

Ricotta toast is the perfect breakfast, light lunch or appetizer. It's very simple yet still elegant enough to serve to any guest. Ricotta is a mild, creamy and fluffy cheese that doesn't have a strong flavor, so it's delicious on a slice of golden crispy toast with sweet and savory toppings.

Instructions
In a large pan, add the olive oil and tomatoes, and heat over high heat. When the tomatoes start to sizzle, reduce the heat to medium-low, and add the garlic. Let the tomatoes cook until they start to soften, about 6 minutes, stirring frequently.

Meanwhile, toast the bread, and put each slice on separate plates.

Use a spatula to mash the tomatoes and mix everything together. Remove the pan from the heat.

Spread a quarter of the ricotta cheese (2 ounces [56 g]) on top of each slice of bread. Place about half a handful of arugula on top of the ricotta.

Spoon a quarter of the tomatoes on top of the arugula. Make sure you get the oil and juice from the tomatoes as well.

Sprinkle flaky sea salt and black pepper to taste on top of the tomatoes, and serve.

PANCAKE MUFFINS

Prep: 0 min
Cook: 25 to 30 min
Total: 25 to 30 min
Servings: 12 muffins

Ingredients
13 tablespoons (100 g) whole wheat flour

1 tablespoon (15 g) sugar

½ teaspoon baking powder

¼ teaspoon salt

1¾ cup (420 ml) low-fat milk

3 eggs

1 teaspoon vanilla extract

Toppings
Whipped cream

Berries of your choice

Maple syrup

Ever since I was little, I've loved pancakes. I remember worrying about whether the hotel breakfast would serve pancakes when I went on vacation with my family. If you're a pancake lover like me, you're going to love these. These pancake muffins are simple and fun to make, and they're perfect to bring to a picnic or a kid's field trip.

Instructions
Preheat the oven to 435°F (225°C).

In a medium-sized bowl, combine the flour, sugar, baking powder and salt.

Add half of the milk to the dry ingredients, and mix until combined. Then add the rest of the milk, the eggs and vanilla, and mix again.

Spray a 12-cup muffin pan with cooking spray, and pour the batter into each cup. Fill each one about two-thirds full.

Bake for 15 to 17 minutes or until all muffins have risen and turned golden brown.

Top the pancake muffins with whipped cream and berries. Drizzle with some maple syrup, and serve.

Note: Serve with a side of fruit to make this more filling. I usually make a fruit salad out of diced apple, pear, banana, grapes and cantaloupe. But you can use any type of fruit you like.

GARLIC AND PARMESAN BROCCOLI

Prep: 5 min
Cook: 20 min
Total: 25 min
Servings: 2

Ingredients

1 (9-ounce [255-g]) head broccoli, cut into bite-sized florets

2 tablespoons (30 ml) extra virgin olive oil

2 cloves garlic, minced, or 1 teaspoon garlic powder

1 teaspoon sesame oil

Salt, to taste

¼ cup (25 g) freshly shredded Parmesan cheese

When a TikTok follower asked what my favorite snack was, I didn't have to think twice. This broccoli is a perfect snack when you get those late-night cravings but want to avoid too much sugar. By frying the broccoli instead of boiling it, you'll get a crunchy texture. The sesame oil brings so much flavor to the broccoli, and the Parmesan topping is perfect for any cheese lover like me. This is also a great side to any main dish.

Instructions

In a large pan, place the broccoli, olive oil and garlic, and stir to combine.

Heat the pan over medium-low heat. Cook, stirring often, for about 12 minutes or until the broccoli has softened but still has a bit of texture.

Drizzle the sesame oil all over the broccoli, and toss.

Transfer the broccoli to a shallow medium-sized bowl, top it with salt to taste, and finish with the Parmesan cheese.

ACKNOWLEDGMENTS

Thank you to all of my fans whose support on social media has made all of this possible. Without you, @simplefood4you wouldn't exist.

Thank you Mom and Calle, for being my biggest fans and always having my back. For inspiring new recipes and helping me out no matter what.

Thank you Dad, for teaching me that hard work pays off. For taking care of everything within a business I know nothing about so I can focus on doing what I love and for giving me your advice and creative ideas.

Thank you Pelle, for putting up with the mess in the kitchen and for cleaning endless dishes. For listening to my late-night talks about all my projects and for always picking me up when I fall.

Thank you Levis, for being the sweetest baby, allowing me to be a working mom.

Thank you Jackie, for introducing me to TikTok. You are the reason I started creating cooking content in the first place, which has led me to where I am today.

Thank you Toni Zernik, for bringing my recipes to life with your creative photos and thank you, Joachim Nywall, for the photos of me in the kitchen.

Finally thank you, Page Street Publishing and Marissa, for believing in me.

ABOUT THE AUTHOR

Alexandra Johnsson is a recipe developer, content creator and self-taught home chef. She's known for her cooking platform @simplefood4you on TikTok and Instagram where she shares short, fun and creative recipe videos. Since publishing her first recipe video in October 2020, her account has grown to be one of Sweden's largest food accounts, and TikTok Sweden announced that one of her recipe videos was the most viewed TikTok video in Sweden in 2021. Her recipes have been featured on large platforms all over the world, such as @foodies (22 million followers on TikTok). *Cosmopolitan* called her Taco Crunch Wrap "the best TikTok recipe in 2022" and the *Independent* called her Chicken Fold Wrap one of "the most popular food hacks on TikTok." When she's not making videos in the kitchen, she's studying for a bachelor's degree in social work, volunteering at a women's shelter and working part-time at a school for children with disabilities.

Alexandra is a multitasker who, before pursuing recipe development and content creation, took classes in psychology and worked as a waitress, schoolteacher, sales associate/clothing retailer and as an au pair. Everyone always asks her how she manages to keep so many things going at once, and to that Alexandra has no good answer other than she loves staying busy.

When she does get some time off, Alexandra loves to travel, try new food and spend time with her family. She's also a soccer player and hobby musician.

INDEX